Forms of Extremity in the Modern Novel

Forms of Extremity in the Modern Novel

BY NATHAN A. SCOTT, JR.

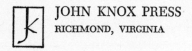

JOHN KNOX PRESS
RICHMOND, VIRGINIA

LIBRARY OF CONGRESS CATALOG CARD NUMBER: 65-21317

© M. E. BRATCHER 1965

PRINTED IN THE UNITED STATES OF AMERICA

9927

To Stanley and Patricia Grean

CONTENTS

EDITOR'S INTRODUCTION

The particular canon that is comprised of that literature which we think of as "modern"—a canon ranging
back to Baudelaire and Melville, and through Dostoevsky and Proust and Joyce and Kafka and Eliot to Faulk-
ner and Malraux and Auden—is a body of art most distinguished perhaps by its radicalism.

There may not, admittedly, be a great deal of political
radicalism in this tradition, and, to be sure, it has tended
to sit rather loosely with respect to the ideologies and en-
thusiasms of leftist politics. But, in this regard, its con-
servatism may well have sprung from the desire to
husband its energies for the immense audaciousness with
which it has wanted to address itself to many other fields
of experience. There is surely no other comparable tradition in literature, for example, that has encouraged the
artist to conceive his own cultural role so assertively.
D. H. Lawrence on one occasion said, "Being a novelist, I
consider myself superior to the saint, the scientist, the
philosopher and the poet. The novel is the one bright
book of life." And one can easily imagine such a poet as
Rilke or such a dramatist as Brecht having been prepared to voice similar claims. Nor is any other tradition
in literature distinguished by such fearlessness in formal
experimentation. The novelist and the poet who, in the

same year of 1922, published *Ulysses* and *The Waste Land* were turning their respective forms upside down, with a kind of dauntless audacity that has constantly marked the modern writer's artistic practice. And perhaps even more notable have been the researches he has conducted into the nature of selfhood, into what it means —in terms of risk and aspiration and suffering—to be truly human: here (as Amos Wilder says of Auden) he has taken "a swarm of spears into his breast. . . . [and] fought through all our issues . . . without adventitious aids or extrinsic authoritarian props."

So it is not surprising that it is in our literature—very much more so than in our philosophy, perhaps even more so than in much of modern theology—that we have gotten the most drastic definitions of the religious crisis of our age. Here it is that we get the most sensitive, and often the most acute, registrations of what is felt to be problematic in traditional systems of faith. And it is also here that we often get the most extreme expressions of the development that Dietrich Bonhoeffer heralded in his famous slogan about the world having now "come of age." For one of the most striking features of modern literature is its lack of hesitancy about improvising into existence *new* principles of meaning and *new* moral norms, in the face of the apparent inefficaciousness of received tradition. Among the writers who are treated in this book, the English novelist Graham Greene stands, of course, for the possibility of an orthodox tradition of religious belief being still available to the literary imagination—but the manifest eccentricity characteristic of Mr. Greene's Catholicism suggests that not even the writer of emphatically Christian allegiance need be expected to be untouched by a cultural climate which tends to promote radically individualist forms of vision and belief. Ours is an age whose mythographers advertise the "death" of God and describe the human situation as that of being perched on a perilously narrow ledge. And John Knox Press has thought it might be useful—particularly for college and university students—to provide for a Christian response to some representative expressions of the kind of "extreme" vision that controls so much of the literature of our time.

Hence it is that this little book has come into existence, along with two companion volumes (devoted to poetry and drama). Here, we are turning to four novelists, all of whom have been profoundly influential in the shaping of contemporary sensibility; and, although these brief essays are not offered in the expectation that they will be found to present any outstandingly original literary explication, it is hoped that they may have some suggestiveness in the indications they give of how theological discrimination can enter into and become a relevant part of one's total response to the important literature of this century.

N. A. S., Jr.
University of Chicago
26 August 1964

I *Kafka's Anguish*

BY NATHAN A. SCOTT, JR.

Erich Heller, in a recent essay on Friedrich Nietzsche, says: "Name almost any poet, man of letters, philosopher, who wrote in German during the 20th century and attained to stature and influence; name Rilke, George, Kafka, Thomas Mann, Ernst Junger, Musil, Benn, Heidegger, or Jaspers—and you name at the same time Friedrich Nietzsche. He is to them all—whether or not they know and acknowledge it (and most of them do)— what St. Thomas Aquinas was to Dante: the categorical interpreter of a world which they contemplate poetically or philosophically without ever radically upsetting its Nietzschean structure."[1] And the range of that literature which Nietzsche interprets "categorically" might well be extended far beyond the confines of the German language, to include the Italian tradition of Moravia and the French tradition of Malraux and Sartre and the Anglo-American tradition of Hemingway and Durrell and Malcolm Lowry and John Hawkes. For the rumor that drifts throughout this entire modern "scripture" is that which was first publicized by Nietzsche, when he announced in his book of 1882, *The Gay Science (Fröhliche Wissenschaft),* that "God is dead."

One of the important critical essays of the nineteenth century is Matthew Arnold's inaugural lecture as Professor of Poetry at Oxford—"On the Modern Element in Literature," which he delivered in 1857 and which he published a decade later in *Macmillan's Magazine*. In this, as in so many of his other critical pieces, Arnold was trying to achieve a clear definition of the essential meaning of "modernity" in cultural history. And if this essay were now to be rewritten, at a little more than a century's remove from the original version, it would surely have to be said (as Arnold did himself to some extent discern in many of his other essays) that the distinctively "modern" element in modern literature—the thing that gives the period's literature its peculiar form and pressure—is the sense that it almost everywhere evinces of the eclipse and the disappearance of God. "Quietly," says Karl Jaspers, "something enormous has happened in the reality of Western man." And this happening which has gradually slouched upon the awareness of the men and women of the twentieth century is one that entails nothing less than the darkening of an old sun, the demise of something that for countless ages had supported and given meaning to human life. The event, as it was defined in the melodramatic language of Nietzsche's *Gay Science*, is nothing less than the "death of God"—the death, that is, *in* the modern consciousness of a sense of nature and history being animated by any Power or Presence or gracious and providential Spirit. "We need a theme? then let that be our theme," advises Conrad Aiken in one of his finest poems: and this is precisely where much of modern literature has found its basic leverage: "it takes its foothold in the fact that we have no foothold,"[2] and the theme that is explored is that (as Aiken says) we are "poor grovellers between faith and doubt" and that our "heart's weak engine [has] all but stopped."

Now, if Nietzsche is the chief "categorical interpreter" of this modern *malaise,* it is Franz Kafka who is his chief counterpart in the realm of imaginative writing. As W. H. Auden remarked a few years ago, "Had one to name the artist who comes nearest to bearing the same kind of relation to our age that Dante, Shakespeare, and Goethe bore to theirs, Kafka is the first we would think of." And this is so, because it is from this remarkably gifted Czech Jew (who died in 1924, at the age of forty-one) that we get what is widely acknowledged to be the most archetypal presentation of the modern hero in the literature of this century: he, so to speak, gives the age away— which is to say that, in the haunting fables of his stories and novels, he makes public a secret nightmare that has been dreamt over and over again, on pummeled pillows everywhere. The man whom we encounter at the center of Kafka's fictions is a creature

> . . . lost,
> Each man lost, in some blind lobby, hall, enclave,
> Crank cul-de-sac, couloir, or corridor of Time.
> Of Time. Or self: and in that dark no thread . . .[3]

"We were fashioned to live in Paradise," says Kafka in one of the notes accompanying the collection of his stories and parables entitled *The Great Wall of China*— "We were fashioned to live in Paradise, and Paradise was destined to serve us. Our destiny has been altered. . . ." And that blunt announcement—"Our destiny has been altered"—summarizes his whole sense of man's condition.

For man does not live in Paradise: he is one who has been ousted from that Good Place where it would delight the soul to be, and his condemnation, in Kafka's vision of the human predicament, is to a world in which he is a stranger and in which he can nowhere descry any reassuring landmarks or any promise of his being ultimately accommodated. In this darkness, there is no thread. "There is a goal," as Kafka says, "but no way: what we call the way is only wavering." Everywhere there is mystery—black, impenetrable, menacing: mystery in the inaccessible interior of a man's own life, mystery in the unbridgeable distances that separate him from his human fellows, mystery in the permanent remoteness of that Castle of Grace the reaching of which would bring joy and healing to the heart's dispeace. So it is a world of fear and trembling—in which (to borrow a figure of Scott Fitzgerald) it is always three o'clock in the morning.

In an early film of Charlie Chaplin's—*City Lights*—the little tramp is picked up by a rich man on a drunken spree and taken back to the man's great mansion, where he is installed as an honored guest. But then, when the man's intoxication has passed, he throws Charlie out of his house. And the relation between these two that is so hilariously chronicled by the movie is one that consists of a long series of reunions and rejections: when the rich man is half seas over, he embraces his little friend and takes him home, putting his splendid house at Charlie's disposal: but, once he emerges from his alcoholic stupor, he flings the tramp out, and Charlie is simply overwhelmed with bewilderment by the caprice with which he is buffeted about. Now the arbitrariness which the lit-

tle tramp of *City Lights* experiences as the governing
principle of his life is something like the senseless fatality
that Kafka's heroes encounter as the sovereign principle
of their own existence. The young protagonist of *Amerika* (Kafka's first novel), for example, is sent away from
home after his seduction by a village girl. But, after his
arrival in this country and his installment in the New
York house of a wealthy uncle, a messenger suddenly
hands him one night his uncle's notification of his dismissal: he has been visiting friends of his uncle's, at their
country house near New York, and, just as he is preparing to return to the city, he is given the envelope marked
"To Karl Rossmann, to be delivered personally . . ." And,
from there on, young Karl drifts from pillar to post over
the United States, being taken in here and ousted there,
as though he were the plaything of invisible and malefi-
cent potencies. But this is what the world is like, in the
Kafkan perspective: it is a place teeming with insecurity
and fortuitousness, asking to be rendered in the slightly
askew scrawlings of a Paul Klee—a world so ordered by
disorder as to make it not at all unnatural for a young
man to wake up of a morning to find himself under sud-
den arrest for an unspecified crime (Joseph K. in *The
Trial*) or to find himself transformed into a gigantic bug
(Gregor Samsa in "Metamorphosis"). Things are ter-
ribly out of joint—and so one is all the time trying in vain
to catch the ear of sinisterly scatterbrained officials, and
one's complaints never reach the right office, and one is
always detraining and yet never quite reaching journey's
end, or one reaches the intended destination but only to
find that one is too late. It is all a kind of ghastly comic
strip, such as might be invented by some infinitely poised

and sober artist miraculously in possession of the gifts at once of Sterne and Picasso and Pascal and Daumier, and the early Walt Disney.

"Our art," says Kafka in one of his Aphorisms, "is a dazzled blindness before the truth . . ." But the difficult question as to what is the general bent and curvature of this "truth" has furnished the subject of one of the great exegetical controversies of modern criticism. It seems generally to be agreed that, however this truth exactly is to be defined, it is of a character at least as complex as the physics of nuclear fission. Yet, though Einstein is reported to have returned a book of Kafka's to Thomas Mann with the comment that he couldn't read it, that the human mind isn't complicated enough, he is perhaps (as Professor Angel Flores has remarked) the only man who has ever admitted his bafflement by this strange and unexampled art. For nearly everyone who has in any way made his reactions to Kafka a matter of public record seems to be absolutely certain not only that *he* has unlocked the secret of what Kafka "really" means but also that he *alone* has found the proper key.

The fascinating diversity of these various "readings" need not be canvassed on this present occasion, but there is one general line of interpretation which does require to be noticed, if—as this essay proposes—Kafka is to be regarded as an exemplary figure not only in the literary but also in the religious history of our time. For there are many of his interpreters who strenuously deny that his fiction is properly to be viewed as belonging to any sort of religious ambiance. They maintain—as in the case, for example, of Günther Anders and his brilliant little book[4]—that what is remote and mysterious in Kafka's

world is not a "figure" of the hiddenness of the Divine
but is simply an expression of how "infinitely" inaccessible the *actual* world of empirical time and commonplace history had come to be for him. And this effort to
"naturalize" the meaning of Kafka's fiction springs from a
rejection of still other styles of interpretation that are, to
be sure, highly dubious. It is motivated, for example, by
an impatience with the attempt that was so frequently
being made a few years ago to interpret Kafka as a sort
of theologian *manqué* who, having misconceived his vocation, adopted a cryptic form of allegorical fiction as his
medium and whose meaning is therefore definable only
as the allegory is translated into the terms of a kind of
"Crisis-theology." But this is an approach than which
none could be more wrongheaded. To handle the work
of one of the great artists of our age in such a way that
its explication becomes merely a matter of notating parallels with the Cabala and the theologies of Søren Kierkegaard and Karl Barth is surely to mishandle it in a
stupidly brutal way. For the business of one who undertakes to talk about imaginative literature is not to hurry
after its presumable *non*-literary sources; and to permit
one's eye to glance off the literary object toward extrinsic
considerations of one sort or another is to forfeit the
chance of saying anything *literarily* relevant about the
work of literary art. And, in Kafka studies, this is a
wrongheadedness that has frequently prepared the way
for still another error—namely, that of regarding Kafka as
a modern Bunyan whose fables record an essentially religious pilgrimage, and a journey that is as decisively
Christian as that which is recounted in the *Pilgrim's
Progress*. But to approach this tortured martyr of modern

agnosticism as a kind of "underground" Christian requires an extraordinary nimbleness of sophistry, and such a tucking away of contradictory evidence as has finally robbed all interpretations in this mode of any truly compelling cogency.

So the opponents of "religious" interpretation are doubtless right in offering resistance to much that they reject. But to grant that a work of literary art is stupidly misconceived if it is approached as an essay in philosophical theology rather than as a work of the poetic imagination and, in this particular case, to grant also that Kafka, far from being any sort of crypto-Christian, is one of the great exponents of what is in many respects a *post*-Christian age—to make these admissions is not to have foreclosed the possibility that, nevertheless, the essential subject of his art has to do with a profoundly religious ordeal. Indeed, to insist, as Günther Anders does, that *The Trial* and *The Castle* concern only a certain curious alienation from the "actual," commonplace, ordinary world of everyday is in fact to blind oneself to the diabolical *irony* with which Kafka occasionally *pretends* that the empirical actuality of the commonplace is the ultimate reality. And it is just in the *ironical* character of the pretense that the religious depth of his skepticism may best be seen.

Stories such as "The Judgment" and "The Penal Colony" and "Metamorphosis" and the novels *Amerika* and *The Trial* all furnish important evidence of what is centrally characteristic of Kafka's vision, but the really crucial case remains the book which in the general consensus is regarded as his masterpiece, the novel on which he began work in the spring of 1922 and which, though not completely finished at the time of his death, was posthumously published for the first time in 1927 under the title *Das Schloss, The Castle*. And, once this remarkably brilliant tour de force is in view, what one wants, inevitably, first of all to remark is how strange it is that so profound a sense of mystery should be evoked in us by a novel whose surfaces are so limpidly clear and apparently uncomplicated. The plot is of the slenderest possible sort. A young man—whose name consists of but one letter, "K."—comes into a village. We do not know from whence he comes, or indeed anything at all about his past. He is identified only as a land-surveyor, and as one who believes he has received a professional appointment from the village's executive authorities who govern the community from a great castle situated on a hill overlooking the little hamlet. But no one in the village appears to have been expecting his arrival, and he quickly discovers that there is no prepared place for him. So his task soon becomes that of winning some clear certification from the Castle that he does in fact bear this appointment and that he has his "place." But it is just this "nod of recognition" that proves exasperatingly difficult to attain, for the inner workings of the Castle represent bureaucratism run wild, and establishing any kind of contact with the officials is a matter of almost infinitely complex protocol, involving documents and proofs and dossiers and endless reams of "papers."

So complex is the "method" of the Castle that K. is soon thrown into doubt about his ability ever to secure any unambiguous statement of his position. Indeed, the further he presses his "case" the more does K. find the Castle to be simply one huge question mark, a world cloaked in the darkest mystery, impenetrable even by the permanent residents of the village who, when they undertake to speak of it, invariably end by contradicting themselves and one another. They do not even agree about which roads lead to the Castle and which do not, so that about all it is possible for K. to conclude is that some roads lead to the Castle and some do not: but, as to which of the roads are used by the officials in traveling between the Castle and the village, it seems impossible to say, for "now one of them is in fashion, and most carriages go by that, now it's another and everything drives pell-mell there. And what governs this change of fashion has never yet been found out." So much at variance with any commonsense view of things is the world of the Castle that it is even impossible to predict what its officials will look like from one day to another: their very physical appearance is constantly changing. Klamm, for example, who is highly placed in the Castle hierarchy, "after having his beer . . . looks different from what he does before it, when he's awake he's different from when he's asleep, when he's alone he's different from when he's talking to people . . ." And the inhabitants of the village can never agree about "his height, his bearing, his size and the cut of his beard . . ."

So this young man who, at the beginning of the novel, seems to come out of nowhere, with no home of his own, with no past, with no memories, is in a dark wood—into which we feel he may have stumbled simply because his life has had no foundations, because he has had no real home and no deep allegiances. But what he wants no longer to do is to continue to live without foundations, and the entire plot of the novel might be regarded as gathering its coherence from K.'s effort to base his life on what he now conceives to be its ultimate Foundation: yet the depressing discovery that he makes is of the remoteness, the distance, of this ultimate Foundation. Having discovered after his arrival in the village that he has no definitely assigned and generally acknowledged place in its scheme of things and that, if he is to prosper there, he must obtain from the Castle a formal certification of the appointment that he believes himself to have received, he never ceases to seek this confirming word. He encounters obstruction upon obstruction and hindrance upon hindrance: and his difficulties are not merely serial, in the sense of following upon each other—they are also interlocked, and they tower upon each other. Each contact that he succeeds in establishing with the Castle— his liaison with the former mistress of an official, an occasional letter received from a minor functionary, a telephone conversation overheard, the two young men who are sent to be his assistants—each contact at first appears to be promising and to hold out the hope that he will finally manage to gain confirmation of his appointment as the village's land-surveyor; but they all prove to be worthless in the end.

Yet K. is incapable of resignation, and he never relaxes in his effort to penetrate to the center of the ultimate Mystery and to wring from it a kind of evidence or validation of his right to exist. He keeps his hope that a direct confrontation with the Castle's chief executive is possible, and one that will result in a clarification of his destiny. The possibility that things are ultimately organized upon the basis of a principle of arbitrariness wounds him so deeply that he refuses to accept the notion of it.

And yet the fact of it never ceases to stare him in the face. For all his encounters with the representatives of the Castle seem to make a mockery of his striving, and, indeed, from the standpoint of the villagers, they are all figments of his imagination. "You haven't once . . . come into contact with our authorities," they tell him. "All those contacts are merely illusory, but owing to your ignorance of the circumstances you take them to be real."

But, while he is suffering the indignity of employment as the janitor in the village school (a temporary job accepted to "make ends meet"), he receives a letter from Klamm, who tells him: "The surveying work which you have carried out thus far has my recognition. . . . Do not slacken in your efforts! Bring your work to a successful conclusion. Any interruption would displease me. . . . I shall not forget you." And, from this, it would appear that there is truly some possibility for K. of a direct relationship with the Castle; but it somehow never quite comes off, and he never gets anywhere at all.

The universe, then, that is exhibited in this book is a dreadful phantasmagoria: it is a universe of insecurity and of uncertainty, presided over by an ultimate Authority, but an Authority to the nature of which the Protestant conception of the religious enterprise, at least as it is conventionally understood, is quite irrelevant. For K. cannot be his own priest: he cannot reach this ultimate Authority without benefit of mediation: there is no possibility of the direct and immediate vision. The Castle is, at every point, surrounded by impenetrable mystery, and this mysteriousness is a sign of the elusiveness of the truth, of the ultimate truth, of the truth that would be a joy and a gladness to the heart could it but be appre-

hended. So the human situation, as Kafka describes it, is
essentially that which Pascal describes in the 72nd Frag-
ment of the *Pensées,* where he says: "We sail within a
vast sphere, ever drifting in uncertainty, driven from end
to end. When we think to attach ourselves to any point
and to fasten to it, it wavers and leaves us; and if we
follow it, it eludes our grasp, slips past us, and vanishes
for ever. Nothing stays for us. This is our natural condition, and yet most contrary to our inclination; we burn
with desire to find solid ground and an ultimate sure
foundation whereon to build a tower reaching to the Infinite. But our whole groundwork cracks, and the earth
opens to abysses." And it is the anguish suffered by man
as a result of this cracking of his groundwork that con-
stitutes K.'s great burden.

K., then, is alone, utterly alone: he is the foreigner, the
outsider, the alienated man, the man pressing his nose
against the glass and wanting to come in, yet being per-
petually baffled and thwarted and confused as to where
is the door that might grant him entrance. Now, to be
sure, he lives in a state of alienation from the community
of the village, from the world of his human neighbors:
there, on that level of things, he is unincluded, uninte-
grated. But to define his isolation in exclusively infra-
human terms—as do many of those critics who deny the
presence in Kafka's fiction of any significant religious element—is not only to take an incomplete view of that isolation but it is also to be unable finally to account for it.
For K.'s estrangement from the villagers is a conse-
quence of his inability to make contact with the "higher-
ups" in the Castle: he cannot win a secure position in the
human order—in the world of his mistress Frieda, and

Pepi the little chambermaid at the *Herrenhof,* and the landlady of the Inn by the Bridge—until the Castle grants him a validating guaranty of that position. So he faces unswervingly toward the Castle—and, for him, it stands not merely for some possibility *within* the human order of settling one's secular affairs, one's citizenship and occupation and residence: no, in the logic of the novel's design the Castle is, for K., the source of the ultimate and absolute truth about himself and his human condition; it is the source *outside* the village, *outside* the world, of any capacity that a man may ever hope to achieve of living satisfactorily *within* the world. And the great fact about the Castle is that it is closed, and inaccessible to the human pilgrim—an infinite perpendicular from the starless heavens, intersecting the incommensurable plane of man's life in concrete, historical time. Thus it is, as Erich Heller says, that "Kafka represents the absolute reversal of German idealism. If it is Hegel's final belief that in the Absolute truth and existence are one, for Kafka it is precisely through the Absolute that they are for ever divided. Truth and existence are mutually exclusive."[5]

So K.—like the hero of *Amerika,* the hero of *The Trial,* the hero of many of Kafka's stories—faces the future always with misgivings, always with mistrust, and always with infinite longing. For between the dreary inanity of daily existence and the Radically Significant there yawns an unbridgeable chasm. And if we try, therefore, to systematize the understanding of reality that knits Kafka's poetic economy into a coherent whole, it must be said that the term which renders with technical accuracy the human condition, as he pictures it, is the term *existence* which, in its most literal sense, means "standing-out-from." For this is indeed what Kafka takes the human situation to be—a standing-out-from, or away-from, or in-separation-from, the Ground of reality. It is the lesson that at many points is enforced upon us by the narrative of *The Castle*, and most especially by the account that is given of the relation between Klamm and the landlady of the Inn by the Bridge. She says to K. in one of their conversations: "Klamm once chose me as his mistress, can I ever lose that honour? . . . Three times [he] sent for me, but he never sent a fourth time, no, never a fourth time!" And she asks K.: "Why should he have concerned himself about me, or better, how could he in any case have concerned himself about me? . . . The fact that he had ceased to summon me was a sign that he had forgotten me. When he stops summoning people, he forgets them completely. . . . And it's not mere forgetting, it's something more than that. For anybody one has forgotten can come back to one's memory again, of course. With Klamm, that's impossible. Anybody that he stops summoning he has forgotten completely, not only as far as the past is concerned, but literally for the future as well." But then she asks: "Where is the man who could hinder me from running to Klamm if Klamm lifted his little finger? Madness," she says, "absolute madness, one begins to feel confused . . . when one plays with such mad ideas."

Now it is clear that, for the landlady—though she was with Klamm only three times, and then the affair was at an end—this remains the most important event of her life. After it was over, she married her husband Hans— but, as it were, half-heartedly, the great experience of her life having now been lived out to its conclusion. Indeed, the sweet memory of it is the only thing that now makes the humdrum monotony of her life endurable. But the fact that the most real event of her life belongs to a brief moment in the past, the fact that now, in the present, she is completely out of contact with Klamm—this bespeaks how great a distance it is at which life has to be lived from that which gives it meaning and significance. "When he stops summoning people, he forgets them completely." And the fact that Klamm "forgets" means that no secure and stable relation with the Castle is possible: to be sure, the woman "surrendered," unlike Amalia, one of the girls in the village, who angrily refused a sexual proposal of Sortini, one of the Castle's high officials, and who, in so refusing, called down upon herself and her whole family the wrath of the Castle and of the entire village. The landlady "surrendered," but the act of surrender did not itself make possible any closure of the hiatus between the divine and the human: it simply rendered it just barely tolerable.

But it is precisely the impossibility of any closure of this hiatus that K. cannot accept. So he resists the landlady's testimony. He insists that the idea that Klamm forgets "is a legend, thought out moreover by the girlish minds of those who happen to have been in Klamm's favour." The landlady's husband is a dull, stupid man, and, when she thinks of what she has had with Klamm, she cannot regard the phase of her life that is formed by her marriage as having any importance at all: in it surely there is, as she says, "no trace . . . of Klamm"—no trace, that is, of anything divine. But K. is prepared to imagine that in some mysterious way Klamm may him-

self have arranged the liaison, simply in order that, being
married to so unimpressive a man, his former mistress
might not be disinclined to come to him, should on some
future occasion he desire to summon her again. "But,"
says the landlady, "it's next to madness to imagine that
Klamm could have given me such a man as Hans as a
husband simply that I might have no great difficulty in
going to him if he should summon me sometime again."
And it strikes her as next to madness to imagine such a
thing, for to do so is to suppose that Klamm had really
not forgotten; it is to suppose that there is some possibility of living with confidence and certainty in a stable relationship with the Transcendent: but to play with such
a notion is, in her view, utterly absurd and "next to madness"—and it is to be remembered that she is an ini-
tiate, she is one who has "surrendered."

K. will not, however, accede to any doctrine or view of
life that posits nothing other than absolute ambiguity at
the heart of things. He knows, of course, how remote is
Klamm, the Castle's principal. Yet, all the while, he expects that, by reason of having taken as his mistress a
girl who was once Klamm's mistress, he will, through his
relationship with Frieda, be able to strike some sort of
agreement or understanding with Klamm. To the landlady, though, K.'s plan is the sheerest nonsense, and she
is careful to remind him that his only chance of getting a
"nod of recognition" from the Castle is by way of the
protocol of Momus.

Momus—this namesake of that Son of Night whom the
Greek gods authorized to find fault with all things—is
Klamm's "village secretary." "Herr Momus," as K.'s land-
lady explains, "is Klamm's secretary in the same sense as

any of Klamm's secretaries, but his official province . . . is confined to the village. . . . That's how it's arranged," she says; "all the gentlemen in the Castle have their village secretaries." And it is in this official role, as Klamm's secretary and as a writer of depositions, that Momus bids K. to give a report of his activities in the community. He proposes to keep a strict record on K. for Klamm's files— not because the record will ever be read by Klamm, but simply, as he says, "for the sake of order." And yet, though in all likelihood Klamm will never see the file on K. that Momus is preparing, it is the only means by which K. can hope to gain access to Klamm, for, at least, it will be put into Klamm's village register: more than this none can say.

But K. wants something more than this: he does not want to trust his fate to the depositions that Momus is taking, for he cannot bring himself to accept the notion that the ultimate determination of his destiny rests on something so provisional, so uncertain. Yet no less doubt-ful a prospect is ever offered. So—like the protagonists of Svevo's *The Confessions of Zeno* and Musil's *Man Without Qualities* and the two tramps of Beckett's *Godot* and the Joseph of Saul Bellow's *Dangling Man* and many another modern hero—this poor derelict, finally, can do little other than "wait," and, in his waiting, there is as much of dread as there is of hope. For his residence is in a world where the dominant experience is of the distance and the absence of God. And it may well be just their commitment to such a world that accounts for why it is that the heroes of Kafka's novels are today so generally regarded as presenting *the* crucial instances in our litera-ture of the twentieth century's characteristic *malaise*.

For ours, as Paul Tillich once remarked, "is a time of waiting; waiting is its special destiny."[6] And even believers have fallen under the sway of our period's most powerful myth—the myth which speaks of the "death" of God, or (put less melodramatically) of the death in ourselves of any power to affirm many of the ways of thinking about God which belong to the received traditions of religious faith in the West. "It is," as Heidegger says, "the time of the gods that have fled and of the god that is coming. It is the time of *need*, because it lies under a double lack and a double Not: the No-more of the gods that have fled and the Not-yet of the god that is coming."[7]

Heidegger's way of formulating the matter may, in its stylistic aspect, be marred by the characteristic heaviness and turgidity of Teutonic philosophy: yet it has the merit of reminding us that the kind of sensibility that is expressed in so much of the art and literature of our age is, for all of its religious negativism, wrongly assessed, if it is simply interpreted as "sheer undialectical atheism."[8] For to assert the absence of God, to assert that God is nowhere to be found amongst the phenomena of the world, is really (in a term of Professor Ronald Gregor Smith's coinage[9]) to "de-divinize" the world. And it may well be that it is only when the world is seen as "sheer world," as a place distinct from God—it may be that it is only when the world has thus been radically "de-divinized" that the question of God can then be truly asked, for this ultimate question concerns "men as having to do with what is not themselves, with what they do not and never can possess at all, as part of their self-equipment or as material for their self-mastery."[10] The question of God, in other words, concerns "what comes to . . . [men] all the time from beyond themselves":[11] it is the question of the Ground of our ultimate dependence, it is the question of grace—and this is a question that can never be powerfully asked until the profound ontological indigence of the world has been radically faced.

So, because of considerations of this order, it is necessary that we approach, with great care and with great tact, much of the extreme religious negativism in the literature of our period which is so perfectly instanced in the novels and stories of Franz Kafka. A novel like *The Castle* or a play like Beckett's *Godot* does, to be sure, exhibit man as inhabiting a radically profanized world and as "waiting"—waiting perhaps for some great disclosure of meaning and grace that will "redeem the time." But it is to be remembered that, as Paul Tillich says:

> . . . although waiting is *not* having, it is also having. The fact that we wait for something shows that in some way we already possess it. Waiting anticipates that which is not yet real. If we wait in hope and patience, the power of that for which we wait is already effective within us. He who waits in an ultimate sense is not far from that for which he waits. He who waits in absolute seriousness is already grasped by that for which he waits. He who waits in patience has already received the power of that for which he waits. He who waits passionately is already an active power himself, the greatest power of transformation in personal and historical life. We are stronger when we wait than when we possess. When we possess God, we reduce Him to that small thing

we knew and grasped of Him; and we make it an
idol. Only in idol worship can one believe in the possession of God.[12]

And, if in this passage Dr. Tillich is approaching the real
truth of the matter, it may just be that such an artist as
Franz Kafka, for all of the wintry bleakness of his land-
scape, can be for us something like what Heidegger calls
a "shepherd of Being"—one, that is, who, by the very
resoluteness with which he plunges us into the Dark,
precipitates us out of our forgetfulness, so that, in a way,
our deprivation of the Transcendent brings us into
proximity to its Mystery, and the distance of the Castle
becomes itself a kind of witness to the Indestructible.
This is not, of course, in the case of Kafka, to gainsay the
testimony of those critics who deny the presence in his
work of any sort of genuinely *affirmative* religiousness:
for that indeed is hardly to be found. The question is not
to what extent his work, by being tucked in here and
stretched there, can be made to yield religious meanings
of a positive and affirmative kind, for it would seem clear
that this kind of adjustment can be accomplished only on
the basis of misguided or dishonest interpretation. The
question is rather to what extent, after the full stringency
of his nihilism has been acknowledged, that nihilism can
itself be religiously appropriated as a discipline of pur-
gation—and this is perhaps the most truly serious question that we are asked to face not only by the fiction of
Kafka but by much of the most representative literature
of our age.

NOTES

1. Erich Heller, "The Importance of Nietzsche," *Encounter,* Vol. XXII, No. 4 (April 1964), p. 59.
2. Stanley Romaine Hopper, *The Crisis of Faith* (New York: Abingdon Press, 1944), p. 119.
3. Robert Penn Warren, *Brother to Dragons* (New York: Random House, 1953), p. 7. By permission.
4. *Vide* Günther Anders, *Franz Kafka,* trans. by A. Steer and A. K. Thorlby (London: Bowes & Bowes Ltd., 1960).
5. Erich Heller, *The Disinherited Mind: Essays in Modern German Literature and Thought* (Philadelphia: Dufour and Saifer, 1952), p. 172.
6. Paul Tillich, *The Shaking of the Foundations* (New York: Charles Scribner's Sons, 1948), p. 152.
7. Martin Heidegger, *Existence and Being,* trans. by Douglas Scott *et al.* (Chicago: Henry Regnery Co., 1949), p. 313.
8. Ronald Gregor Smith, "A Theological Perspective of the Secular," *The Christian Scholar,* Vol. XLIII, No. 1 (March 1960), p. 22.
9. *Ibid.,* p. 21.
10. *Ibid.,* p. 15.
11. *Ibid.*
12. Paul Tillich, *op. cit.,* p. 151.

II *Hemingway and Our "Essential Worldliness"*

BY JOHN KILLINGER

The deaths of few men—kings and presidents and great warriors mainly—have produced the kind of mourning which followed the announcement on July 2, 1961, that Ernest Hemingway had killed himself. It had been widely known that he was in failing health, but it was rumored that he was hard at work on something which might prove to be his *magnum opus*; and it seemed almost inconceivable that the man who had come to be identified both in his writings and his public life with the theme of courage and dignity in the face of violence and suffering and death should end it all by putting a double-barreled shotgun into his mouth and pulling the trigger. For a long time he had flirted with death; at last he had married it.

Some of the ingredients in the formula that made Hemingway a great writer are discoverable and some are not. He had a profound respect for truth. Like Albert

Camus, he was impatient with writers who are willing to write lies, or to talk about things they have not experienced. He was more than once accused of "living it up in order to write it down." To an amazing extent, he managed to write only about the things he had known and which had become distilled into his own blood and bone. This gave an innate consistency to everything he wrote, and guaranteed that no matter how many imitators there were they could never match him on his own subjects.

The language he used was of course an ingredient. Robert Penn Warren has said that Hemingway did for Anglo-American prose in the twentieth century what Wordsworth did for the poetry of the nineteenth. André Maurois wrote that "A Hemingway novel was to the traditional novel what functional architecture is to ornate architecture."[1] He had an unsparing contempt for all forms of cant and hypocrisy, in speech as well as in life. As he told the old lady in *Death in the Afternoon,* a lot of writers simply talk manure—though he used a much stronger Anglo-Saxon word for it. When he was writing well, he had an uncanny predilection for the *mot juste,* the right word, which was always old and simple, never florid or noticeable; it became a transparency through which the object itself was seen. He had a way of evoking the right response, of making you *feel* what he was writing about, whether he was doing dialogue or describing a mountain pass with pine needles banking it softly on either side and a cortege of soldiers moving through it.

His kind of writing was never easy, of course, and he managed it only by discovering certain rules for working, which became inviolable habits. One was always to stop at a point when he knew what he would write next, so that he would not have trouble getting started the next time. Another was to look long and hard at any adjective he had written and to strike it out if he could not truly defend its use. Still another was to begin the day's work by writing one true sentence. Getting that sentence was often the hardest part. He said that he would stand at the window of his apartment in Paris, the one where Verlaine had once lived, and gaze over the rooftops of the city, thinking, "Do not worry. You have always written before and you will write now. All you have to do is write one true sentence. Write the truest sentence that you know."[2] Finally he would get the sentence, and then go on from there. If he found later that it had not been so true as he had thought, if it had been ornamental or unreal, he would cut it out and start with the first simple declarative sentence he had written.

He was singularly of his own time—of the time that produced Woodrow Wilson in politics and Sigmund Freud in psychoanalysis and John Joseph Pershing in the military and Reinhold Niebuhr in theology. Specifically, it was World War I that proved to be the real catalyst in his development. He was severely wounded while delivering chocolate to the soldiers at the front in Italy—doctors picked two hundred and thirty-seven metal fragments out of his body. In a sense, he never got over the trauma of that wound. It seemed to him to be the microcosmic focus of the whole mad disaster that was befalling young men and old countries all over Europe. It became his vantage point, from which all other experiences and ideas dropped away into mere foothills and valleys, organizing life and life's values into an inevitable system of ordinates and subordinates. His whole *Weltbilt* formed around that single occurrence, bifurcating the world's population into those who have seen death at close hand and have learned to live gracefully in its presence and those who have only smelled it at a distance and have behaved badly, retreating into illusions and complicated emotions. Looking back on the time when the Closerie des Lilas was crowded with veterans who had lost limbs or eyes or whose faces had been reconstructed, leaving them iridescent or shiny, he said that in those days they did not trust anyone who had not been in the war. They were a race of men set apart by violence and horror.

Hemingway even interpreted his past in terms of what had happened in the war. His first volume of short stories, *In Our Time* (1925), consisted of narratives about his early initiation into violence, such as the time he watched his father perform a jackknife Caesarean on an Indian squaw and was then ushered quickly away because the squaw's husband had slit his throat while it was going on, or the time his father got in a row with a tough half-breed he had hired to cut some logs and there was almost a fight but there wasn't because his father walked away—all interspersed with some of the clearest, steeliest little sketches of the macabre scenes of war ever written. Nick Adams, the main character of the stories, was patently Hemingway himself, and in the later stories he was having a lot of trouble digesting what had happened in the war. The war was easily the biggest thing in or out of his consciousness. In the last story in the volume, the one called "Big Two-Hearted River," Nick was clearly suffering from shell shock, and was going off alone to fish, trying to get hold of himself by being close to nature. The earth itself reflected something of his problem—it was hard and the grass was burned over—but there was shade by the water and the water was cool and dizzying and he enjoyed the fishing.

The same theme, amplified, became the basis of his first novel, *The Sun Also Rises* (1926), which definitely established him as a first-rate writer and justified the years of penury and hard work in Paris. The protagonist of the novel, Jake Barnes, is merely an extension of Nick Adams; only this time he has been wounded in such a way as to render it impossible for him to make love to a woman. Perhaps this special touch was the influence of T. S. Eliot's popularization of the fisher-king myth, which was so ready a symbol for a time of apparent impotence. Jake compares himself to the steers which are run in with the bulls to keep them docile. There is a great deal of night life—drinking and fighting and talking and making love—among the expatriates pictured in the novel. But the phrase from Gertrude Stein which Hemingway set at the front of the book, "You are all a lost generation," has led to the somewhat general misunderstanding that the book is only about the profligacy of the postwar generation. It is about that, to be sure; but it is also about the earth and its riches, as contrasted with man and his follies. The second inscription which Hemingway used, the one from Ecclesiastes which included the title phrase, begins, "One generation passeth away, and another generation cometh; but the earth abideth forever." In a sense, this was really what the story was about. It was an answer to Gertrude Stein. It was always Hemingway's answer: man has a lot to learn, but the earth has much to teach. The only thing was, he could not sound too much like Thoreau in writing about the earth because our time had experienced something Thoreau and his time had not fully dreamed about—the war. So he showed us the lost generation scrambling around Europe and finding its only real health in the trout streams and at the bullfights and wherever it could get back to what was whole and elemental. He was working out his own therapy by writing about it.

"Your psychoanalyst?"
"A portable Corona, No. 3."

In his next novel, *A Farewell to Arms* (1929), Hemingway moved from the protagonist as victim to the protagonist as hero. The hero was still a wounded man—Lt. Frederic Henry was, in fact, wounded almost precisely as Hemingway himself had been—but he had begun to develop a philosophy about what was happening to him. In one notable passage he rescued some ants on a burning log, only to steam them to death by pouring water on the fire, and then railed fiercely against the great impersonal "they" which thus idly governs the destinies of men. It is a telling protest against the conventional notions of God and his mercy. Henry is convinced of the absurdity of war and of the world in general, and decides to make a "separate peace"—which is in reality a no-peace, a decision of permanent rebellion not unlike that of Camus' Sisyphus.

There was still some confusion in Hemingway's mind, however, as to what the rebel's responsibility is for other men who are cosufferers with him in the world. In *To Have and Have Not* (1937) he made Harry Morgan, the extremely tough and renegadish hero, decide in the end that "a man alone ain't got no bloody f—ing chance," and in *For Whom the Bell Tolls* (1940), a novel about the Spanish civil war, he let Robert Jordan, the American ex-schoolteacher turned revolutionary, surrender his life guarding the escape of a nondescript band of Spanish rebels. The hero was of necessity a rugged individualist, eschewing the intricacies and politeness of ordinary social relationships, but he was also somehow involved in the total human situation, and could not quit it simply to save his own skin. Again in these two novels, though, the hero was a wounded man, and the "code" for heroism, as the critics called it, was becoming tighter and tighter.

With the publication of *Across the River and into the Trees* (1950), the code was complete. It had, in fact, somewhat overpowered the rambling data of real life, from which novels are usually made, and had become concretized into a sort of formulistic hero named Colonel Cantwell. The reviewers and critics were extremely hard on the novel. As Joseph Warren Beach said in an article entitled "How Do You Like It Now, Gentlemen?"[3] Cantwell was the oldest of the avatars of Nick Adams but not so certainly the most adult of them in his attitude toward himself. It was not hard for anyone to tell that it was Hemingway himself peering out from behind the masque of the old soldier he musedly named Cant-well. Personal allusions abounded in the novel, including the fact that Cantwell was fifty years old—Hemingway's own age at the time of the writing. In a way Cantwell was the code hero as distinguished from the regular hero; that is, he represented the quintessence of everything the regular hero strives for but does not necessarily reach. The story is his *Liebestod*. He knows he is going to die. He has returned to Venice to say goodbye to many things he loved, including duck-hunting in the marshes, making jokes with the *Gran Maestro* at the Gritti Palace Hotel, and embracing a very young countess while drifting along in a gondola. Like Hemingway, he was wounded as a young man, and that and subsequent wounds had been his greatest teachers. On his way into Venice he stops his driver, gets out of the car, finds the exact spot where he first received the wound, and goes through a strange little ritual memorializing the place. He completes his mission in Venice, all along giving many close-ups of the code hero, and then dies in the car as it speeds away from the city.

In his preoccupation with death, or with "grace under pressure" as he called it, Hemingway displayed a certain basic kinship to the German and French existentialists, for whom death is also the great reductionist, simplifying life to its most elemental forms. Cantwell's stance, the one on which the novel depends, is very similar to Martin Heidegger's concept of *das Sein zum Tode*, in which a man finds authenticity for the self by consciously anticipating his own death. Hemingway doubtless worked out his own personal equation for this from his war experience and his days at the Closerie des Lilas and other cafés where the veterans gathered, and was in no way dependent on Heidegger, as Sartre and other existentialists admittedly were. He may, however, have derived something from reading Dostoevsky, who made a classic use of the facing-death theme in *The Idiot*. Hemingway was greatly captivated by the Russian novelist, and could not understand his friend Ezra Pound's complete dislike for him.

Wherever he got it, this became the Hemingway formula: Take a good man and put him in a hard situation, preferably one involving suffering or violence or death. If he is really good, if he is capable of integrity, he will suddenly begin to see life in its bolder, truer outlines, and any false values he has acquired from a conventional rearing will start to drop away. The lines of force in his life will become visible to him and he will play them for all they are worth. He will abandon all pretensions, even those he tends to fool himself with. He will, in a word, become the individual, the true man, the hero. And he will be especially fond of war and bullfights and big-game hunting, where he can continue to see death and to give it and in so doing experience over and over the catharsis he needs to be what he is. His business is pretty well stated in a phrase which Hemingway used to describe Romero's style as a toreador in *The Sun Also Rises:* "the holding of his purity of line through the maximum of exposure."

There are two or three corollaries to the formula.

One is that the man who has passed through the valley of the shadow of death becomes strangely sensitized to the beauties of the earth. Like Sisyphus returning from the underworld, he knows better than most men how to appreciate the wonders of life. He has a sense of form, of style, by which he attempts to categorize and hold his sensual experiences. He has a way of discovering little rituals by which he "fixes" the variegated impressions he receives during his lifetime. Malcolm Cowley, in his introduction to the Viking Portable edition of Hemingway, said that Hemingway has provided us with rites for drinking (in *The Sun Also Rises*), for animal sacrifice (in *Death in the Afternoon*), for sexual union (in *For Whom the Bell Tolls*), for self-immolation (in "The Snows of Kilimanjaro"), for conversion (in *To Have and Have Not*), and for symbolic death and rebirth (in the Caporetto passage of *A Farewll to Arms*). One might add, since the publication of *Across the River and into the Trees,* the ritual for death itself. And there are countless other little rites that have to do with eating and fishing and sailing and shooting and talking and cursing and writing—in short, with nearly everything Hemingway ever did. In the story "Big Two-Hearted River," Nick Adams discusses the "correct" way to make coffee on a campfire and the "correct" way to bait a hook, as well as the "correct" way to fish. And once he climbs out of the waters and sits on the bank to smoke a cigarette so that he won't "rush his sensations any."

This preternatural sensitivity, stylized into ritual, suggests that there is a kind of mystery about life and the universe for Hemingway, a certain vibrant quality going beyond the mere realm of the senses. As a writer, he had first to get what was there for the senses—to accumulate the data—but, taken together, they amounted to much more than a series of unrelated impressions and responses. Hemingway's universe is occasionally described as a flat one, lacking the dimension of thickness, as though he reduced everything to the visceral level. But I have known few persons either in print or in real life with such an exquisite openness to wonder and excitement. One frequently finds him, in a novel or a documentary piece, savoring life like a small boy with gooseflesh. More than many casual readers have realized, he has dealt in the wildness and imprecision of life, in the mysterious forces which transcend or go too deep for human understanding.

One could cite, for example, the strange shadows enveloping the saloon of "A Clean, Well-Lighted Place," waiting beast-like to devour the old man when the place is closed and he must go out into the night. Inside, one hears the incantatory eeriness of "Our nada which art in nada, nada be thy name" and "Hail nada, full of nada"— the invitation to nothingness which threatens internally in the story what is waiting externally. The mood is unforgettable. There is something haunting about it that will not go away, that will not lie quietly in the mind.

Or remember how old Santiago in battling his great fish in *The Old Man and the Sea* calls the fish his brother. This is obviously more than a slight case of pathetic fallacy. It is like the realization of kinship between the torero and his bull in the moment when he is putting the sword in. It is the kind of recognition of the inner unity of all life that puts one in mind of St. Francis of Assisi, who spoke that way to all the birds and animals and trees.

We could recall Hemingway's unhesitant confession of superstition, both personally and in his characters: how he crossed himself before getting onto the main road with a reckless driver, in *The Dangerous Summer;* how Brett and Jake prayed even though they didn't feel like it, in *The Sun Also Rises;* how all of them, Nick Adams and Jake Barnes and Lt. Henry and Hemingway himself, were afraid of the dark; and how Santiago promises, even though he is "not religious," to say ten Hail Marys and ten Our Fathers, if he catches a good fish, in *The Old Man and the Sea.* All of this, in spite of Hemingway's passion for accuracy, for recording the way things are. He is incurably romantic and primitive—even religious. More than most men, he is keenly aware of the dark and subterraneous currents roiling just a few feet from where we stand at any given moment. A man who has faced death or great suffering sees these things.

Another corollary to the basic formula—it must be our last one here—is that traditional concepts of the Divine are often meaningless to the man who has faced death in the twentieth century. The erosion of faith has pretty well taken place. Jake Barnes still goes into old cathedrals to pray, but his prayers soon deteriorate into sleepy monologues about his good wishes for the bull-fighters and his desire to get some money. It is obvious that the rites of sacrifice in the bullring are much more dramatic and compelling to him than the crucifix in the sanctuary of the church. He regrets that he is "such a rotten Catholic," but does little to improve the situation. Count Greffi, in *A Farewell to Arms,* asks Lt. Henry if he is *croyant.* "Only at night," is the reply. Only at night—when the mind is not well ordered and the racial unconscious is strongest. "We do not have God here anymore," says old Anselmo in *For Whom the Bell Tolls,* "neither His Son nor the Holy Ghost." Anselmo reverts to prayer after he discovers the massacre that has been made of El Sordo's men on the hilltop; but God still seems embarrassingly out of place to him in this modern setting.

As a candidate for the ministry, I was once counseled by a well-meaning professor in graduate school not to spend too much time on Hemingway—that Jeremy Taylor and Lancelot Andrewes and other great Anglican devotionalists were much more suitable to form the temper of a young ecclesiast. It was an understandable caution, but hardly an appropriate one. No one with a proper feeling for the mystery of God and its opaqueness, its imperviousness, will be put off by the apparent "atheism" of Hemingway's writing. He does not really derive from Feuerbach and Nietzsche, as has been claimed. The irrepressible joy of Zarathustra's announcement of the death of God is missing in him. There is instead a kind of mournfulness, a weight of grief. Hemingway's personae are never exultant at having lost God; they simply see the loss as the way things are. Most of the time they are really sorry about it. Hemingway treats the hardness of things without God, and the consequent stoicism with which men must resist the forces which would crush them. In *The Old Man and the Sea*, for example, a sadness, a melancholia, echoes on every page like some immemorial sorrow soughing in the cradle of the waves: Santiago plainly misses God. Hemingway's characters are not concerned, like Nietzsche, with becoming the *Übermensch*—they only want to be human. But they cannot accept the incongruousness of a fifteenth-century deity in the catastrophic world of the twentieth century.

It took great personal courage for Hemingway to write of God as he did, and he has done us a greater service than we realize. The truth is that he may do much to sharpen the Christian's vision of the world he lives in and to help him to be faithful to the profounder strata of his religious commitment. The God he has slain is only a God who has deserved to be slain. The honesty with which he faced the contemporary religious situation is—or should be—a welcome curative to an unfortunate kind of supernaturalism quite popular in any age, whose God just floats around up in the wild blue yonder without really seeming to be in touch with things. "I never felt sorry about losing God," said Anne Dubrueilh in Simone de Beauvoir's *The Mandarins,* "because he had robbed me of the earth." Precisely! That God should have been lost. The real God does not rob men of the earth at all; he enables them to possess it more truly. Hemingway's men and women, always more sentimental than those of de Beauvoir, do regret losing God; but they will not let him stand in the way of their having the earth. The strong humanistic dynamism in them will not let them believe finally in any misshapen deity who blocks the path to their self-realization as creatures of the world. They must, though regretfully, set him aside.

It is surprising, when one first realizes it, how very compatible all of this is with the ideas of certain modern theologians, particularly Tillich and Bultmann and Bonhoeffer, who have expressed a deep concern for having a Christianity that is a Christianity of the world and of the age and that is not merely a disconnected philosophical idealism. It was Bonhoeffer who coined the phrase "the essential worldliness of Christianity," and who later sealed his relationship to New Testament faith with a martyr's death in a Nazi prison camp. These highly intelligent theologians have all taken issue with the kind of etherealism or spectralism which tends to be identified as the Christian faith in the minds of many people. They plead for a return to the world as the only way to reinvest the concept of Incarnation with real meaning. Without a true sense of earthiness, the idea of an enfleshed God quickly becomes a mere obscenity, a perversion dangerous in its one-sided emphasis. In the tradition of the Reformers, who taught us the trick, we have always written "The Word became flesh"—flesh with a small "f," as though it were of subordinate importance in the union. This is Hellenism at work; it is not Hebraic at all, or Christian.

Hemingway, along with other modern writers, rediscovers the earth to us and helps to validate to our thinking the meaning of the Incarnation, and of the God for whom Luther said the world is a veil and a vestment.

One thing that probably puts more Christians off than anything else in their approach to Hemingway is the apparent libertinism of his characters. They drink a great deal and spend a lot of time at the races and at bullfights, they take an unusual pleasure in giving out death, and they are unequivocally *à la moderne* in their views of sex and its uses. Hemingway himself pretty well distilled the flavor of this criticism in his first novel: "You're an expatriate. You've lost touch with the soil. You get precious. Fake European standards have ruined you. You drink yourself to death. You become obsessed by sex. You spend all your time talking, not working. You are an expatriate, see? You hang around cafes."[4]

But this surface approach misses entirely the inner order of Hemingway's experiences, the sense of discipline and severity in personal behavior which was his own before it was his characters' and then was theirs if he respected them and considered them part of the real brotherhood, the confraternity of honor. He does not have a conventional morality, it is true; but neither is he guilty of moral nihilism. He has abandoned the traditional morality only in order to establish a truer, more intimate one, one following the subtlest contours of a man's private existence instead of merely covering him, like a factory-cut suit, from the grosser indecencies. No

one ever required more of himself or his characters than
Hemingway did. His incredible sense of responsibility for
right behavior is discoverable in any of his heroes, but
perhaps it is strongest in Cantwell, the bronzed old soldier of *Across the River and into the Trees.* Everything is
de rigueur for Cantwell. He even reproaches himself for
having failed to turn out an electric light when he left his
hotel room, and he refuses to pick up a parcel from the
hotel desk until he has seen the clerk and paid him for it.
His young friend Renata asks him if everything must be
so hard. "With me, I guess," he says.

Hemingway had little use for people who did not hold
this kind of rein on themselves. They were "messy" people, like the horrible fisherman who rented Harry Morgan's boat in *To Have and Have Not* and then lost Harry's tackle by not fishing according to the correct form.
He was especially disgusted by fakers in the bullring,
showmen who merely dazzled the tourists by seeming to
approximate danger but without ever actually being
near it. His own accolades were reserved for that special
breed of torero who had got so used to looking at death
that he always seemed to be seeing something way beyond you when he looked at you—the fighter who genuinely worked just a hair's breadth away from disaster
and defied the steel-hard horn in the groin or along the
small of the back. This kind of man had what the Spanish
call *pundonor*—which Hemingway in *Death in the Afternoon* explained to mean "honor, probity, courage, self-
respect and pride in one word." Hemingway always
found the work of such fighters "beautiful," "lovely,"
"true." He said of one toreador in *The Dangerous Summer* that he worked as gracefully as if he were serving

Mass in a dream. Integrity and form were united; honesty became style. And style was Hemingway's finest surrogate for religion, his nearest approximation to that peculiar quality describing the authentic man or the new creature in Christian theology.

Time will probably vindicate the judgment that of all of Hemingway's works *The Old Man and the Sea* represents his major achievement as a writer. There are many who would hold out for *A Farewell to Arms* or *For Whom the Bell Tolls* as his high-water mark, and in either case there is much to be said for the choice. But in *The Old Man* Hemingway was getting back to the length of piece where he first won mastery and was probably most often at his best. Many of his longer books were marked by a kind of unintentional serialization; here there was less problem of sustaining the tension. Moreover, he was in *The Old Man* attempting to refine his favorite theme—that of the courage and dignity of an individual "holding out" against impossible odds—into a classic or mythological statement. The superb spareness of that work, with one old man battling the sea for his great fish, every word just so, the prose as lean as the old man or the fish's white spine, is unrivaled in modern letters. It is like Sophoclean drama, played as it was meant to be played, in the out-of-doors.

What Hemingway has accomplished in *The Old Man,* whether he meant to or not,[5] is an incredible interweaving of the particular and the universal. He has managed to reunite certain important symbols of the Christian faith (or of almost any faith)—the sea, the fish, the cross—with their primeval sources, reviving in power and eloquence figures which had to some extent become arid and dumb.

The sea, as the all-encompassing fact of the setting, is Auden's "enchafèd flood," the deep that calleth unto deep, the mysterious cradle of all life. The fish, so vividly real and engrossing in the story, is also symbolic of primitive forms of life. And the cross, the mast borne up the hill by one whose hands have been lacerated in the struggle with the fish, a struggle he has both won and lost, is hardly the cross of old Santiago alone, but of man without a face, without a home, of man generic and enduring and longsuffering. There is a sense of the *mysterium Tremendum* about this story, as of the sea's having become a vast cathedral for the enacting of life's oldest and most important liturgy. It is hardly the work of a shallow or irreligious man.

Even Hemingway's death had a dimension of depth to it. Beyond the basic fact of suicide, it carried undertones of being a ritualistic participation in the death of his father, who had also taken his life years earlier. Clarence Hemingway had been a successful physician in Oak Park, Illinois, and was apparently a much adored father. Ernest had had a difficult time accepting the fact that his father had died by his own hand. It seemed to classify him with malingerers and cowards. Robert Jordan, in *For Whom the Bell Tolls,* repudiated his father for having killed himself. He said that if he and his grandfather ever met his father in another life they would not speak to him. He carried the gun his father had used for that unspeakable act up high into the mountains and threw it into the deepest part of a cold, still lake. But Freud was too shrewd to be caught in a lie here: Hemingway was irresistibly drawn to the memory of his father. And, in the end, he went the way his father had gone, initiating himself into the final mystery by the very means he had seemed so to abominate. The religious implications are obvious to anyone reflecting a moment on the strong patriarchal motif in Judaism and Christianity. In a way transcending conscious reflection, he was fulfilling a basic law by honoring his father.

Of course reading Hemingway is a great deal different from reading Taylor and Andrewes and the devotionalists. Nevertheless, there is a strange kind of saintliness about this modern writer—an integrity and a transparency so unusual as to put him beyond the ordinary categories of religion and irreligion. In his later years an exceptionally sensitive portrait of him appeared on the cover of *Life*. I framed a copy of it and had it hanging on my wall for two or three years. His face and head were marked by various scars and bumps collected in a lifetime of adventure. His face was sort of ashen, with the veins standing out prominently in delicate shades of blue and red, and there was a soft, chastened look about the eyes. He looked like some medieval saint, a large man but lean from fasting, and with his mind on things clean and spiritual. That is a good look to have, and a hard one to come by. Hemingway had earned it by years of self-discipline, of refusing to be less than honest or to settle for less than the truth about men and existence. He was not unworldly at all; in fact, he was about as this-worldly as a man can be. But in his own way he discovered the kind of secular sainthood that even Christian theologians are beginning to discover and to praise—the kind that doesn't separate a man from life in order to make him a saint or remove him from the world in order to find God.

NOTES

1. "Ernest Hemingway," Carlos Baker (ed.), in *Hemingway and His Critics* (New York: Hill and Wang, 1961), p. 44.
2. Ernest Hemingway, *A Moveable Feast* (New York: Charles Scribner's Sons, 1964), p. 12.
3. *Sewanee Review*, LIX (Spring 1951), pp. 311-328.
4. *The Sun Also Rises* (New York: Charles Scribner's Sons, 1925), p. 118.
5. Hemingway once said, "Read anything I write for the pleasure of reading it. Whatever else you find will be the measure of what you brought to the reading." Cf. George Plimpton, "Ernest Hemingway: The Art of Fiction," *The Paris Review*, V, No. 18 (Spring 1958), p. 76.

III *The Christian, the Saint, and the Rebel: Albert Camus*

BY WILLIAM HAMILTON

Christians writing about literature have often been justly accused of offering moral homilies instead of authentic criticism. Moral homilies are in disrepute among some Christians, but this is too bad, because we really are very confused morally, and need all the good homilies we can get.

This is by way of confessing that I am setting out deliberately to offer a moral homily based on some of the writing of Albert Camus, and underplaying, virtually ignoring, the usual functions of literary criticism. This procedure may, in a curious sense, be faithful to Camus' intent, for some have claimed—Sartre is one—that Camus' fiction doesn't really belong in the category of the novel at all, but rather stands in the tradition of the Voltairean moral tale.

I am further limiting myself by making use of a portion of Camus' total work: my main interest will be in the novel *The Plague* (1947). I shall also call upon some material from the "philosophical" work that serves as an interpretation of *The Plague—The Rebel* (1951), and also from that moving and fragmentary address to some Dominican monks that appeared posthumously in *Resistance, Rebellion, and Death* under the title "The Unbeliever and Christians" (1948).

I do not wish to overstress the arbitrary character of my choice of material. This material is, I am persuaded, the center of Camus' work and stands as his most typical and in some ways most influential writing. Concentration on this limited area means I will make no attempt to present Camus' literary and moral development as a continuous story with a plot. We perhaps need only recall that his earliest writing is influenced by the physical climate of his native North Africa and contains moving words of praise of nature's healing power. Camus breaks into European fame with his first novel, *The Stranger*, which led him to be loosely identified with the postwar existentialist movement. The nonfiction book of essays from the same period that is useful in interpreting *The Stranger* is *The Myth of Sisyphus*. It is a study of suicide and the meaning of absurdist existence. The plays *Caligula* and *The Misunderstanding* belong in this period as well.

The next period is that with which I am here concerned, the period of *The Plague*, *The Rebel*, and the play *The State of Siege*. Rebellion has replaced absurdity as the central ethical term, and Camus is well beyond his existentialist mood. He tries to face candidly some of the baffling ethical problems of the postwar world. It is this Camus that a whole generation of young men and women since the war has studied with care, and it is this morally sensitive Camus, rather than the novelist, surely, who was given the Nobel Prize in 1957. His accidental death deprived us, to be sure, of an interesting stylistic experimenter, a good novelist, but not a great one. But his death deprived us, unquestionably, of a lucid moral voice, a kind of conscience for many of us who had lost or forgotten what consciences we once had.

The postwar American reader, then, read Camus, and still reads him, for largely nonliterary reasons. He reads him not so much for pleasure or delight, but for guidance. The classical guides of family, church, and school have for the most part dwindled into vacuousness, and we must catch our moral guides on the run. If a novelist happens to serve us, so be it; we will not be put off by the litterateurs who frown at our shamelessly American and moralistic use of literature. For in our country today, it still is blessedly the case that not everyone wants to grow up voting for nice candidates, reading *Time* and discussing its improbable contents with friends at parties, throwing up in the morning before going to the office as the psychic price of being paid well for useless work. *The Plague* by Camus has been, can be, and should be used to illuminate this fissure in the gray flannel curtain.

I am choosing this particular Camus material for some brief comment because in it he tells us most exactly what kinds of choices are possible for us in the kind of world we have stumbled into. *The Plague* is a novel about the interaction between three types of life, three models: the Christian, the saint, and the rebel. The author is least involved, interested, and accurate in his portrait of the Christian; he most identifies with the rebel, but there is a deep affection that he cannot help showing for the figure of the saint. I wish to look at his portrait of the three characters, which are also portraits of three ways of life.

In *The Plague*, bubonic plague has broken out in the North African town of Oran. We can study what Camus takes to be the Christian response to this crisis in the first sermon of Father Paneloux, the learned Jesuit priest. The sermon is a reasonably accurate portrayal of the orthodox Christian attitude to suffering and evil, with a strong overtone of the Deuteronomic view. The plague is God's deliberate judgment on the people, the priest declares, a judgment they have fully deserved because of their sin.

Dr. Rieux, the novel's narrator and Camus' spokesman for the virtues of rebellion, comments after the sermon that he does not take Paneloux's remarks too seriously, as Christians are usually better than their words. As the plague progresses, the priest comes to take a more active part in the fight against it, and he clearly moves to a practical understanding of the meaning of suffering at variance with his conventional sermon.

The crisis for the priest comes as he and Dr. Rieux witness together the death of a small child. The agnostic doctor, in his weariness, blurts out that the child was innocent and could not be taken as a sinner being punished by God through the plague. The priest is somewhat taken aback by the doctor's head-on theological attack, and suggests that perhaps men should love what they cannot understand. The doctor refuses this piety, declaring that he will never love a scheme in which children die horrible and premature deaths. Again the priest attempts to Christianize Rieux's rebellion, saying that as a doctor he is really working for man's salvation. But again Rieux refuses the priest's importunity. No, he says, man's health is my goal; salvation is a big word I have never understood.

The two part amicably, but the author has clearly given the exhausted doctor the better of the exchange. The priest has been directly attacked, even if graciously and gently, for his answer to the problem of suffering.

Rieux hates Paneloux's assurance that the plague is God's judgment. In a later sermon, the priest has clearly been deeply influenced by his experience with the plague and especially by his encounter with Rieux. The second sermon proposes, both in its tentative style and in content, a quite different solution to the problem of suffering from the early confident and conventional one. This new solution is partly agnostic in tone; there are many things we know, and there are some things we do not know. The suffering of sinners we can understand, but the suffering of children we cannot. But, Paneloux says, do we give up our faith just because there are some hard parts to it? The love of God is a hard love, and it requires utter surrender, all or nothing. If we have no answer to the special problem of the child's suffering, we can stand, the priest concludes, with our backs to the wall, disclaiming easy answers, and point to the suffering of the man on the cross. Instead of an answer, which the first sermon had offered, the priest now refuses to solve the problem and asks for submission to the mysterious will of God, whose ways are past finding out.

Father Paneloux is a rather wooden character in the novel, and his Christianity, both in the unsatisfactory first sermon, and in the more convincing second one, is a rather stiff affair. Camus is really offended by it, even in its revised form. The author's relation to Christianity, dramatically worked out in the scene between Rieux and Paneloux, is spelled out in a most interesting way in the fragments from the address to the Dominicans I have already referred to.

Camus stands before the monks as an unbeliever and as a rebel. But, he tells them, he does not accuse Christianity of falsehood or illusion; he simply states that he cannot accept it. What he seems offended by is the unwillingness of Christians to enter into dialogue with unbelief. It is not that they are wrong, apparently, but that they are timid and dishonest. "What the world expects of Christians," Camus says, "is that Christians should speak out, loud and clear" so that no one can possibly doubt that they are willing to take a stand, to pay up, and if necessary to get hurt. Behind this indictment is, of course, the fact of the papal agreements with Naziism and Fascism in the earlier days of this century.

Combining these actual words of Camus with the protest of Dr. Rieux against Father Paneloux, we come up with a two-part indictment of the rebel against the Christian. First, the Christian is accused, because of laziness or fear, of keeping silence on the momentous issues of justice and freedom. Second, if he is not afraid, he is accused of explaining evil away, by positing some eternal harmony, and thus taking away the need to overcome present injustice. Camus did a thesis on St. Augustine when at the university, and often refers to that other

North African's frustration in being unable to find the source of evil. Camus admits that the source or explanation of evil cannot be found, and he very nearly says it ought not even to be sought, for even the search pre-empts the actual mitigation of evil in the real world. This is nicely put by Dr. Rieux when he remarks that he would rather cure than know, as if the search for understanding took away somehow the desire to cure. This points to a deep irrationalist streak in Camus; it is perhaps Algerian rather than French.

He concludes his remarks to the Dominicans: we may not know how to explain evil, but we know what to do. Perhaps we cannot so remake the world that children will never again be tortured, he says, but "we can reduce the number of tortured children." If Christians, he concludes rather bleakly, lose the virtues of rebellion and indignation that have in better times marked them, then, he says, Christians will live but authenic Christianity will die. What does he want of the Christian? Not a clearer intellectual strategy, but a sustained and powerful voice, interceding, along with others, for children and for men.

Camus' view of Christianity is radically ethical, and Christian health is identified with speaking out, breaking silence, entering into the critical issues of the day on the side of the oppressed. In securer times, we might charge him with a too narrow, not theological enough, understanding of Christianity, but today I think we probably should allow him his attack. In the encounter between the Christian and the rebel, Camus raises two issues, or, more exactly, three: *one,* the problem of a just solution to the problem of suffering (the difference between the first and the second sermon of Father

Paneloux); *two*, the silence of the church in the face of evil (the accusation in the 1948 speech); and *three*, the relation between one and two: if you explain evil successfully, won't you give up the fight against it? Here is a sophisticated, and by no means settled, indictment against Christianity. Will not the Christian have to move much closer to the world of the rebel before any satisfactory answer can be given to any of these three issues? Can a Christian movement toward the world of rebellion be justified, tolerated, even imagined?

In the novel, the foil to Dr. Rieux who really interests Camus is not Father Paneloux at all, but the curious, shadowy, and appealing figure of Tarrou, who works with the doctor in organizing the campaign to control the plague. Tarrou does in fact represent Camus' way of dealing with the religious problem. He is the man who is not content merely with fighting, curing, rebelling. He is more than the rebel who affirms his solidarity with the earth, and with the defeated. What that "more" is, however, and just how the vision of Tarrou differs from that of Rieux, the author has not made wholly clear.

We can see what Camus wanted to do. In *The Rebel*, we recall his approving citation of the famous cry of Van Gogh, that though he can do without God, he cannot do without something that is greater than he is, which he calls "the power to create." As we carefully read Rieux's meditations after Tarrou's death it becomes clear that when Tarrou describes himself as a saint without God, Camus does intend to assign to Tarrou something that goes beyond the world of the rebel. The rebel is the man who is content with earth and human love. Tarrou and the saints without God have aspired somehow beyond the rebel's goal, but—having refused a conventional religious or mystical interpretation of that "somehow"—Tarrou doesn't really shape up as radically different morally from Rieux himself. After Tarrou's death, Rieux meditates, and note the deliberate imprecision of the language: "But for those others who aspired beyond and above the human individual toward something they could not even imagine, there had been no answer." Camus' saints are not fixed on God; the admirable fools like Paneloux cover that field quite adequately. The secular saints like Tarrou, it is clear, know even less peace at the end of their lives than do those who have opted for human life and love.

So, it seems, the saint is the man who walks the way of the rebel, and a little bit more. He is perhaps slightly more interested in understanding, in comprehension. ("Comprehension" is the word Tarrou mysteriously used once to describe his moral code.) But Tarrou's search for understanding is not rejected by Rieux, as is the Christian's search, which, we may recall, is severely attacked as a concealed escape from the task of fighting evil. The irrelevance of Christian explanations of suffering is an unshakable conviction of both Rieux and his creator. But Tarrou's search for understanding is apparently acceptable to Rieux, perhaps because it is so imprecise and inchoate. Camus seems to intend to distinguish the moral worlds of Tarrou and Rieux. Tarrou is a trifle more objective and passive; understanding, we might say, requires a readiness to receive, a passivity, that will always be irritating to the rebel. The secular saint, committed to understanding the richness and color of a tragic life, is bound to seem to the rebel as indifferent to political realities, afraid, over-intellectualizing. But beyond this, Camus never sharply distinguishes the two moral visions, perhaps because he is quite close to both men, and wants both of them to appear to bear a portion of the truth.

We will turn in a moment to the two very effective scenes between the doctor and Tarrou in which Camus dramatizes for us the tension and agreement between the rebel and the saint without God. We should note first that there is no confrontation in the novel between the Christian and the secular saint. This is a confrontation we will have to imagine for ourselves. I think that the issue between the two, had Camus brought them together in the novel, would have been over the nature of man. Can a man achieve purity in the midst of a radically impure world? The saint, even the secular saint, is a saint precisely because he has to answer "yes" to that. The Christian, with his acute sense of his own sin and thus the sin of all men, answers "no." It may be the Catholic "no" which says, in effect, "withdraw partly from the world, pray passionately for it, do some of its work, but live apart, and you may become perfectly obedient to God, and in that sense a saint." The Protestant "no" differs slightly. There is no purity in the world, and no place outside the world where it can be achieved. Therefore live fully in the world, praise God and love your neighbor there, and call upon the forgiveness of sins to heal your inescapable impurity. In the tension between the Christian and the secular saint, this is the issue. Camus has rejected God, but he has not rejected the possibility of sanctity; his view of man is more optimistic than either the Christian or the secular existentialist one. He makes this very clear in his address to the Dominicans, where he says that while he is pessimistic as to human destiny, he is "optimistic as to man." And the novel is full of this duality—a hatred, disgust, rejection of the world, "the indifference of the sky," along with a trust in ordinary men. At the very close of the novel, this duality is most sharply focused. As he looks back on the plague, and how men have dealt with it, Rieux finds much to admire in the various ways men coped with its ravages, and much to admire in men themselves, but, he adds, there is only suffering, a never-ending series of actual or moral plagues, and no peace, no final victory.

We should not linger longer on this encounter between the Christian and the secular saint. I am convinced that the Christian must come to terms with Camus' confidence in the possibility of sanctity in this world. I think that the transformation of sanctity into work, the change the sixteenth century effected, leading to the once creative and now demonic conception of the sanctity of labor, is no longer an acceptable one, and that alongside doing, acting, shaping, working, the Protestant must somehow learn to wait, to receive, to play, to waste time without guilt, and, it may even be, to be pure and transparent to the God that lies beyond him and his purity.

In the first dialogue between Tarrou and Rieux, Tarrou seems to hover on the edge of things, smiling mysteriously, asking questions, knowing all, agreeing with whatever the doctor says. There is no debate at all, only a kind of interview. Rieux's position is much the same as that displayed in his argument with the priest, referred to above. If I believed in an omnipotent God, Rieux says, I would give up curing the sick, and leave that all to him—exactly as Father Paneloux rejected the doctor's help when he fell ill with the plague. Tarrou doesn't argue with this rather unformed idea of Rieux, and is content to nod sagely when Rieux defines his role as that of fighting against creation as he finds it. This means no successes, no victories. And when Tarrou asks him who taught him all this, Rieux replies, "Suffering."

Later in the novel, Rieux and Tarrou have another talk and in this Tarrou tells a long story about his own past. In this story are a number of reflections of Camus' own autobiography, especially at the point where Tarrou speaks about his fundamental decision, the one that has shaped his life, his decision never to kill, to be an innocent murderer. At the beginning of *The Rebel*, the figure of the rebel is defined as one who has refused to kill. Thus Tarrou, and not Rieux, stands for the rebel at this point.

If Tarrou is the innocent murderer, Rieux is the healer, and the distinction between the passive saint—defined by a refusal—and the active rebel-healer—defined by a fight against creation—again reappears, and may well be the only useful distinction that we can draw between the two men. Indeed, it seems to be the case that the "rebel" of Camus' nonfiction book is really both Rieux and Tarrou, and it might be ventured that rebellion as a general ethical category must be said to include the idea of secular sanctity.

In any case, Camus never really developed the idea of the ethical man as one who refuses to kill. He did move toward a passionate repudiation of capital punishment, but never toward anything like a pacifist point of view.

We are tempted to ask: Is this refusal to kill an absolute ethical stand, from the sophisticated relativist? What is the relation of the refusal-to-kill of Tarrou and *The Rebel* to Albert Schweitzer's "reverence for life"? What is its application to the contemporary problems of war, peace, and weapons?

This is a fundamental point in Camus' definition of "the rebel," to which both Tarrou and Rieux seem to contribute—the rebel has refused to kill, even to participate in those licensed forms of killing that modern life allows. He has thus refused to make history, and is an exile for the stream of history-makers, or killers, or users of power. If one refuses to make history, to kill, what is it that one does? Not, we have already seen, go to God. Why not? Because, as Camus writes in *The Rebel*, "The toiling masses, worn out with suffering and death, are masses without God. Our place is henceforth at their side, far from teachers, old and new." The rebel is a man without God because the victims of history, the defeated, the poor, the masses, are without God, and if the rebel is to stand beside them honestly and helpfully, he must also be without God.

This is an odd and fascinating point of view, and it raises for the Christian some quite fundamental questions about Christian ethics. But we must move on. We have tried to show that artistically the encounter between the rebel and the saint is quite successful in *The Plague*, but intellectually rather confused. We began by setting the two moral images over against one another, and ended by confessing that no really important distinctions could be drawn between them. And we wondered after all whether Camus himself did not intend that the rebel of the nonfiction essay should encompass the novel's "rebel" as well as the novel's "saint."

One can apparently be both a rebel and a saint, though not, as we shall see, a Christian and a rebel. We must draw together and fill out our portrait of the rebel in Camus' thought.

In *The Rebel* Camus is not just setting forth rebellion as one particular style of life among others. It is *the* fundamental ethical category. Indeed, it defines man as man. Rebellion is acceptance of the world, it is the fight against the suffering in the world, it is identification with the victims of that suffering. The individual, rebelling, finds a community, a solidarity with others. I rebel, Camus states, therefore *we are*.

We have already sketched out the encounter between the rebel and the Christian. For the Christian today, this is an important encounter, and for this reason it is unfortunate that Camus is not at his best in portraying it. In *The Rebel*, we ought to remind ourselves, the world of rebellion and the Christian world of grace are defined as mutually antagonistic. Nietzsche is praised for attacking not merely a distorted or idolatrous God, but the God of love himself. So, for Camus, once man questions God, he kills him. Once man questions God, in other words, he departs at once from the Christian world of grace, and becomes a rebel. Any man who questions God can only be a rebel; he cannot be a Christian: ". . . only two possible worlds can exist for the human mind: the sacred (or, to speak in Christian terms, the world of grace) and the world of rebellion." Camus knows a little about

Catholic Christianity, and this is perhaps why he has borrowed its popular all-or-nothing apologetics (either despair or Christ; Christ was either madman or divine, etc., etc.). We saw this sort of thing in Paneloux's sermons in a suaver form, and it makes a very bad argument.

The rebel, we recall, was afraid of the Christian's claim to know, particularly at the point of the problem of suffering. "A man can't cure and know at the same time," Rieux insisted. We'd want to ask "Why not?" but we also need to admit that there are dozens of immoral and irresponsible solutions to the problem of suffering that purchase logical precision at the price of moral insensitiveness and blindness.

If the rebel fears the Christian's attempts to understand and know, he does not fear the saint's longing for understanding, perhaps because there is very little content to that longing, beyond a generalized feeling that there may be more than earth and human love and solidarity with the victims. Tarrou's "beyond" is really just a restlessness and a seeking, and thus not too different from the restlessness of Rieux himself, who had sadly rejected both God and the secular substitutes. So, the rebel says, when the Christian goes beyond earth and man, he tries to become God and he ignores man, or, if he manages to be interested in the victims, it is at the price of not obeying his principles. Any Christian who is socially responsible is thus inconsistent. But when the saints like Tarrou long for the secular "beyond," Rieux can only wish them well, and he neither rejects nor misconstrues nor ignores. For all of his interest in dialogue, Camus really never seemed to experience authentic

Christian dialogue, except apparently with politically confused intellectuals like Marcel, and he apparently never really sought it out. One is tempted to say that it is too bad Camus knew so little about Protestantism and so much about Catholicism.

Thus, the rebel is afraid of the idolatrous element in man, and avoids turning himself into a god, not by confessing a true God, but by leaving the realm of gods altogether as too perilous a moral adventure, and by confessing his desire to be merely a man alongside his neighbors on this earth. Life on this earth will give plenty of "tears of impotence," but the only way to live and die is to join yourself to the earth; the only way to be a man is to refuse to be a god, for Camus is convinced that a man who tries to believe in God cannot stop until he becomes that God. Man's mind, another Frenchman wrote, is a perpetual factory of idols, and this may have been part of what Camus meant. Christians have known enough dehumanized Christians not to be utterly contemptuous of Camus' harsh assurance.

The rebel, at least in his embodiment as Dr. Rieux, is perhaps a little too conscious of his own integrity, too unwilling to allow radically different moral visions to have their own validity. Rieux is the most guilty of this self-righteousness here, Camus least so in his touching address to the Dominicans. (I ought to record my conviction that the few pages of this address are really very close to necessary reading for any member of the younger generation today who wants to see what choosing Christianity entails.) There is, further, a very interesting bourgeois strain in the rebel. "The thing was to do your job as it should be done," Rieux remarks. Hard work, plus compassion for the victims, plus the utter absence of illusions or hope. God and a promise of a successful future have both been abolished from the moral vision of the rebel, because both may blunt the edge of compassion. Faith is abolished for the rebel; hope is quite absent. But love remains; "rebellion cannot exist without a strange form of love."

Rebellion, then, has to do with the most fundamental decisions that we can make. It is about vocation, it is about politics and race. Can it be chosen by those today who have as yet no moral image that contents them? Can it be wedded to the image of the saint, the one who spends himself for others, quite oblivious of himself? Where are the saints to be found today? They are clearly not in the Temple or in the Academy. Are they in the Street? And how can the rebel become Christianized without falling into the insensitive, intellectualistic, irrelevant traps that Camus has set, sprung, and charted? What would a Christian rebel look like, and how would it be possible for him to live with other Christians? And with non-Christian rebels? And saints?

This is the sort of moral homily that *The Plague* seems to elicit today. It is the sort of serious, if nonliterary, question that many have already put to the book and to the author. I do not for a minute suggest that the three-fold triptych of Christian-saint-rebel stands for the only available moral positions today. As a matter of fact, in the novel itself there are at least two other forms of heroism, both of which receive a most sympathetic interpretation from Camus. One is Grand's loyal and self-effacing service to the cause of stopping the plague; and the other is the figure of the journalist Rambert, who had chosen happiness, and whom Rieux refused to condemn, even when Rambert was trying to escape illegally from the plague-ridden city.

We have many moral images claiming our attention today, and a few of them are more insistent, more fashionable, and potentially more successful than any of the three that the novel offers. There is, today as always, the *martyr*. He has some affinity with Tarrou and the idea of the secular saint, but necessary to the idea of martyrdom is the idea of death, giving one's life. Camus does not deal with martyrdom, for though all the people in the city of the plague are risking death, they are not martyrs because they did not choose to stay but were compelled to stay by law. Contemporary Christianity has little room for martyrdom, for it is not dangerous to be a Christian in our world. But somehow even our banal world seems always to find a little room for the possibility of martyrdom, even though there is a literary tradition stemming from Dostoevsky that is profoundly suspicious of the moral health of any martyr. In the civil rights movement, something like martyrdom is taking place, and there will be a good deal more of the young instructing their elders on these matters, one suspects. The martyr needs the danger of death, and one of the reasons the act of martyrdom is so difficult and rare is that we live in a culture that thinks it has abolished both the danger and the fear of death.

The *playboy* is another moral image still holding on in the urban centers of America. It has been popular even with antimoralistic Christians and clergymen, and especially with large groups of young men and women unable to transcend the moral styles of fraternity and sorority life. The fall of the playboy as a way of life, which we are beginning to witness, is not due to the denunciations of the righteous or the religious. These denunciations have been nearly as silly as playboyism itself. It is primarily laughter at it and boredom with it that has begun to cause the decline of the power of playboyism, and the emergence of a few young men and women who have on their minds one or two other matters besides innocent seduction. But the life of the sensualist will always have its appeal; it is encouraged by the structure and ideology of American higher education, and if a magazine editor doesn't come along to provide its marching orders, someone else equally unqualified will.

Related to the saint, though in somewhat sharper focus than Tarrou and the saint without God of Camus, is a moral image that might be described as that of the *fool* or the *jester*. Its mark is not that overpraised virtue, the sense of humor, though there is a good deal of laughter here. Its mark is innocence. The fool or jester is always in contrast to power and success, and his function, as in *Lear,* is to comment on the hollowness of what the conventional world values. Man as the innocent one is to the fore here: the sucker, the fall guy. There is a strain of this in the radical teaching of Jesus; this vision fascinated Dostoevsky, and his Prince Myshkin is a classical portrait of the type. And Christians will always be fairly close to this position (which probably needs a better public relations campaign than it tends to get in our day), whenever they see that at times the world is mastered as well by waiting, receiving, suffering, getting hurt, as by action, politics, and shaping.

The fertile and fascinating power of Albert Camus will

be reported on for a good many years by men of many interests. The specific moral and religious line I have taken is admittedly an incomplete interpretation of the man and his work, and should not be taken as an adequate literary criticism at all. But I believe that I have described a part of the author's intent, and I know I have described the way a whole generation of open and restless young men and women have read, reread, and acted upon the life and work of Albert Camus.

IV *The Vision of Graham Greene*

BY RAYMOND CHAPMAN

Future historians of the novel may well describe the twentieth century as the "age of commitment." The logical irony of time can hardly fail to stick a label on the period in which labeling has been the popular fashion. The majority of readers today are made happy when they can attach a tag to a new author and thus become able to shine in social chat by answering the top-scoring question, What does he stand for? This is the question which usually takes precedence over more disputable matters such as form, style, and the creation of character.

The fashion would not have developed had not the major writers of our time made it possible. It is an age when the old background of belief has been broken to fragments, and the fragments trampled and scattered. If we still think that the novel is important in society, it is reasonable to try to discover what a novelist believes, what position he holds. Graham Greene presents no difficulty here: his Christian faith is made clear in all his important books.

The fixing of a label, however, is not a certificate of good art. Passion and sincerity are not enough, and the man who decides that, since he is a Christian, or a socialist, or a vegetarian, he might as well write a novel in order to disseminate his beliefs, will produce neither a good novel nor effective propaganda. I believe that it is wisely said on Broadway, "If you have a message, give it to Western Union." Yet when a man has the talent to create a good novel, that which he believes is sure to emerge through his work—to emerge not as a result of direct preaching but as a synthesis of the diverse and often trivial details that make up the total effect.

Graham Greene, then, is to be approached not as a Christian apologist but as a novelist of distinction whose work treats largely of Christian characters and themes. In a prefatory letter to a French study of his novels, Greene stated that his writing was motivated by the destinies of his characters, not by a desire to express his thoughts about the problems facing mankind.

It is possible today to describe oneself as a Christian without being accused either of uttering a commonplace or of claiming to be especially good and pious. For Christianity is no longer an accepted concomitant of the ordinary social background, and no one can hold this faith and remain unaware of a certain tension between it and various trends in society as a whole. Born in Berkhamstead, a small town in the south of England, in 1904, Graham Greene was received into the Roman Catholic Church as a very young man, thereby setting himself somewhat apart from his environment. England is a country where practicing Christians are now a minority of the population, and where the greater number of Christians are Protestants. The British are a people distrustful of rigid dogmas and apt to resent any authoritarian regulation of conduct. They also bear a deep-rooted and irrational fear of Roman Catholicism, grounded on historical conflicts but enduring in an age when tolerance had shaded into apathy. (It is, happily, much less marked now than it was a generation ago.)

Many earnest Victorians, like George Eliot, feared that anarchy and immorality would follow the retreat from Christianity: they suffered in trying to equate their own intellectual doubts with the good of society as a whole. In the event, antinomian behavior did not sweep the country, and most people continued to hold a certain code of morals to keep them from excess. As we shall see, Greene has frequently pointed out that this kind of pragmatic, private morality is not enough—a view with which every Christian is bound to agree.

Anyone who swims against the current so boldly as to claim that there is the will of a transcendental deity to be obeyed in one's personal actions, who suggests that the realms of good and evil are not bounded by such simple concepts as unselfishness and good-neighborliness, does not find it easy to get a hearing. The novelist today is not a remote, oracular figure, whose latest pronouncement on questions of the day is awaited with excitement. He is in competition with other media of entertainment that require less intellectual effort than reading a serious book. If he has something to say, he must dress it in a lighter cover. Greene has in fact described some of his novels as "Entertainments," but in all his work he has taken the lesson well to heart: writing with humor, building up the suspense of a strong story, accepting the modern demand for violent action.

Yet in becoming a popular novelist, Greene has not

satisfied all those who share his faith. He has been accused of unorthodoxy, even of treachery to his Church, by depicting sinful and incompetent priests, by making some of his worst villains out of baptized Catholics and some of his saints out of adulterers. He does indeed go to these extremes; but it must be considered that the Christian today is in a crisis situation. Over a large area of Western society, the church is neither obeyed nor persecuted but simply ignored. A Christian writer needs to be violent, to startle people by extremism, if he is to convince them that his faith has a total relevance to the immediate situation.

There are many extremes, inside Christianity and outside it, which can get in the way of the vital existential truth. There are Catholics with a mechanical repetition of devotional exercises as an insurance toward salvation, and Protestants who reduce Christ to a human teacher and hope for salvation through a vague sense of universal brotherhood. The opponents of Christianity seize on these extremes and present them as the norm, drawing out of a ragbag all the abuses which have ever been committed in the name of faith. Or else, with an equal sense of crisis and urgency, they preach their own ideologies as a panacea for the age. Our fragmented society has a thousand voices, a thousand prophets jostling to be heard, all convinced that they could move the earth if they could find a place to stand. Hardest of all to overcome is the dismissal of Christianity as merely an acceptable framework for weddings and funerals, with occasional Sundays, but nothing more. Overwhelmed by violence in the secular field, society believes that religion at least is safe and tame.

Greene has written for a society accustomed to violence, in his political thrillers and stories of espionage, as well as in his more important work. Yet while depicting the instability and violence of the world in which his people live, he is more concerned with the conflicts within the characters themselves. For him, as it must be for all who call themselves Christians, the salvation of the individual is of tremendous and literally cosmic importance. It is to be attained not by an accumulation of good deeds or a repetition of pious exercises but through an inner struggle to reach that perfection of personality which is offered by Grace. Thus the Christian may find himself in conflict not only with the world in general but even with the church as an institution. The same theme appears in the novels of François Mauriac, with the English translations of which Greene was associated when he worked in a publishing firm. He has acknowledged his debt to Mauriac and to another Frenchman, Charles Péguy, who held that the sinner was at the very heart of Christianity, fulfilling and understanding it better than anyone except the saint. A quotation from Péguy to this effect forms the epigraph of Greene's novel *The Heart of the Matter*, and Péguy himself is cited in *Brighton Rock*, though not by name, as an example of a man attaining sanctity through sin. It is an idea which is fundamental to Greene's work.

Greene's characters, then, are neither saints nor heroes in the conventional sense. The heroic age in literature is over: we are familiar now with the "little man," the antihero who enlists our sympathies by being as fallible and incompetent as ourselves. The novelist no longer presents an image of virtues which we can admire but can probably not go far toward attaining. The postwar British novel has seen a spate of these antiheroes: Amis, Braine, Murdoch, Wain, and others have made their principal characters reflect the sickness and self-seeking of the society in which they live. Greene has been doing this for rather longer.

Pinkie, the young gangster in *Brighton Rock*, is typical of a generation that has grown up without roots, without loyalties, the target of false promises that society never fulfills, twisted and embittered by disillusionment before he has become a man. Greene stresses the power of this disillusionment to become a driving, destructive force. Pinkie is a puritan, hating drink and sex, seeking to keep his own inverted integrity untouched by others. Like the great Romantic Outsider, the Byronic rebel, he walks alone in the wilderness. Yet even his crime and violence are petty and ultimately self-destructive, for he lives in an age that lacks scope not only for the great hero but also for the great rebel. The Satanic roar of defiance is now a whimper on Brighton Pier.

Many of Greene's characters show this same failure either to adjust to society or to triumph over it. They are lacking socially, professionally, or personally, some of them bearing a physical defect to announce their failure in a society that judges by externals. The priest in *The Power and the Glory* is a drunkard; Anthony in *England Made Me* is a waster, with a scar caused by his own incompetence; Scobie in *The Heart of the Matter* is passed over for promotion; Rycker in *A Burnt-Out Case* is a failed priest; Maurice in *The End of the Affair*, a writer dissatisfied with his achievements, is lame; Smythe, the militant atheist in the same book is disfigured; Raven in *A Gun for Sale* has a harelip.

These failures and defects emphasize the loneliness of Greene's people. They are the very types of the present age, showing the isolation of the individual. Those of his characters who are exiles in the literal sense stand for the alienation of modern man from the stability that society seemed to promise when it was whole. We have no real homeland in this world, but are as cut off as Tench the English dentist languishing in Mexico, as Minty in Stockholm, and Harris in Africa, clinging to their old school photographs. Nor is faith any security against the inner loneliness, for even here the self may rebel and create an exile through its rebellion. Scobie in his adulterous love is forced to abstain from Communion:

> The priest had reached Louise in his slow interrupted patrol and suddenly Scobie was aware of the sense of exile. Over there, where all these people knelt, was a country to which he would never return.

The background against which the characters move is a drab one, tarnished and grubby. Greene can highlight the tawdriness of a world filled with cheap glitter, that false impression of luxury which destroys good taste and real craftsmanship: a world of cheap hotels and saloon bars, of night clubs and amusement parks. Our "little man" feels flattered and pampered when he is being worst exploited. More than this, the seediness of Greene's world is yet another way of emphasizing the seedy incompetence of his characters.

For Greene, like Henry James, has a gift of using symbols which help to create the character who sees them, which become part of the reader's understanding. To take but one example, the police official Scobie feels his experience in images of law, judgment, restraint, and punishment. Often the very setting of the background becomes like an extra, comprehensive character in the story, exerting its influence. This is a rare gift, which Greene shares with masters like Balzac, Zola, and Hardy: the description of the seafront in *Brighton Rock* is as significant in its way as the brooding introduction of Egdon Heath in *The Return of the Native*.

Long ago, the city was an image of peace and safety, walls built against the lawlessness without, a very analogue of the City of God. Nowadays the city can be a shabby hell, the seat of growing evil like Isherwood's Berlin or a place of the restless dead as in *The Waste Land*. Greene can give this feeling, and he needs no exotic setting: in *A Gun for Sale*, Nottwich is made a terrible place, but it is recognizably the Midland city of Nottingham where he worked as a young man.

Another image has been changed in recent years. It used to be accepted that childhood was a state of purity and innocence, like man before the Fall. A careful study of many Victorian novels reveals darker things beneath the surface, but few writers overtly showed infantile corruption until Freud revealed the jungle that is raging behind the pink face in the cradle.

Greene is fascinated, almost obsessed, by the early loss of innocence. He sees life as a journey in which more experience brings more evil, the sorrow that comes through knowledge. One of his recurring characters is the child-woman, able to do harm because she has a woman's power with a child's disregard of consequences. In her fall, older men are made the unwilling instruments of corruption. Such are Milly Drover in *It's a Battlefield*, Marie Rycker, Helen Rolt, Anna Hilfe in *The Ministry of*

Fear, who looked "too young for all the things she must have seen." Most pathetic of all is Pinkie's bride Rose, willing to damn herself for love of an evil that she cannot comprehend.

Greene's own childhood was not happy, and he has revealed some of the images of horror which afflicted him when the dark night came over him too young, as it does over Pinkie and Raven. Pinkie, hating sex because he saw his parents' joyless, aggressive intercourse, tells the story of a young pregnant girl's suicide almost exactly as Greene relates it elsewhere as a fact of his own hearing when a child. Raven is brutalized by his institutional childhood, and those characters who have been to expensive boarding schools are little happier in their memories.

Now it may well be asked how we can claim as a Christian writer one so preoccupied with seediness, failure, and hatred. The answer is perhaps in the title of an early novel: *It's a Battlefield.* The world is at war, a mortal struggle fought not by angels in shining armor but by the ordinary people of ordinary towns. Greene pulls theology off the shelves and declares it as the Articles of War. "Reasonable" men over the last hundred years have tried to shrug off religion, joining Samuel Butler's call for a life of continual moderation and compromise. Greene insists that the Christian is in the thick of the fight, an extremist among the pessimists and nihilists, suffering like them but with a greater hope. He eschews the robust optimism of earlier Catholic writers like Belloc and Chesterton, preferring the different kind of joy found by Kierkegaard, "in danger, over seventy fathoms of water, many miles from all help."

God is the hunter, Francis Thompson's Hound of

Heaven. If you run away, he tracks you down and confronts you in your last loneliness, like the Mexican priest who does not want to be a martyr but cannot escape, like Sarah in *The End of the Affair*, a saint against her will, like Scobie, held by the images of faith even in his suicide. Once the fight is joined, no one can choose how far he will go. "There are no limits," says Huxley's sardonic Arch-Vicar in the barbaric society of *Ape and Essence*, and Greene could echo those words in his own way. Like Newman, he regards the act of faith in God as so tremendous and complete that nothing else is a real problem; so Sarah Miles feels:

> I believe there's a God—I believe the whole bag of tricks, there's nothing I don't believe, they could subdivide the Trinity into a dozen parts and I'd believe. They could dig up records that proved Christ had been invented by Pilate to get himself promoted and I'd believe just the same. I've caught belief like a disease. I've fallen into belief like I fell in love.

This is extremism indeed, unlikely to commend itself either to unbelievers or to careful, "reasonable" Christians. Yet who can dare to say that God demands less than all?

Once the great acceptance is made, other things all seem insignificant. Greene's treatment of indulgence in drink and sex shows how little they touch the real problem. They are only palliatives against the inner terror, the fear of meaninglessness that Paul Tillich has described as the special dread of this modern age. Many novelists, freed from the prudish restraints that caused imbalance in nineteenth-century fiction, now give a whoop of delight and fall into as bad an imbalance on the other side. Greene is concerned not with the fact that people get drunk and commit adultery but with the reasons why they do so. To concentrate on these things as of primary importance in themselves is to accept the values of a very unsatisfactory world.

For the world has its values, and they are concerned more with externals than with the inner self. Here we come, to make use of another of Greene's titles, to the heart of the matter. Men without God still try to make up their own rules, but these are limited, constricted rules that have no final sanctions and are easily broken. "The not done things are done every day," says Maurice in *The End of the Affair*. Life within faith is not the narrow, frightened thing that many believe it to be and some try to make it; it is a new freedom, a greater responsibility, a fresh dimension within which to act and suffer. The Church accepts the idea of "natural law," but only as something incomplete in itself and to be transcended.

Greene continually attacks "morality" as the world at large understands it. Morality is the god of people like the Lieutenant in *The Power and the Glory*, a predictable god, ensuring that certain acts will be followed by certain consequences. Good intentions may have some force, but they do not always lead to better results than bad ones on the secular plane. Scobie is a good man, noted for his sense of justice, but he sinks to degradation and suicide through trying to do the right thing for everybody.

Greene's fullest exposition of the real nature of the conflict is given in *Brighton Rock*. Ida Arnold has the

morality of secular society—easy, kindly, setting little
value on chastity. Her brief encounter with Hale,
Pinkie's victim, inspires her with a desire to avenge the
murder. Like a plump, affable Fury, she hunts down
Pinkie to his death: justice is served and society is re-
paired where a gash had appeared on its smooth features. Yet she is really playing in a different league from
Pinkie, never touching or even comprehending the real
lower depths. Pinkie and Rose, the lapsed Catholics,
know differently. Ida pleads with Rose to save herself by
betraying Pinkie:

> "I know one thing you don't. I know the differ-
> ence between Right and Wrong. They didn't teach
> you *that* at school."
>
> Rose didn't answer; the woman was quite right;
> the two words meant nothing to her. Their taste was
> extinguished by stronger foods—Good and Evil.
> The woman could tell her nothing that she didn't
> know about these—she knew by tests as clear as
> mathematics that Pinkie was evil—what did it mat-
> ter in that case whether he was right or wrong?

Those who launch out on the deep in Kierkegaard's
way take the greater risk in pursuing the greater hope.
Sometimes Greene's regard for theological standards
comes near to despising the lesser values for which they
should stand on guard. "There are no limits": this is true
of evil as well as good, and there is no more cruel and
bitter ending to an English novel than the last sentences
of *Brighton Rock* when Rose goes away from confession
to hear for the first time the words of loathing which
Pinkie had spoken on a gramophone record when she

asked for a loving message. The Church may transcend
natural law, but she does not abrogate it; she would
hardly approve of Scobie's action in breaking his duty as
a Government official by conniving at a Portuguese cap-
tain's smuggling of a letter. Yet Greene seems to suggest
that the fact they are both Catholics makes an extra-
legal bond between them.

There is a weakness here perhaps, but Greene is surely
right to emphasize that the totality is more important
than the details. Christianity is not a set of rules or precepts, but a commitment to a Person. The precepts are
there and not to be ignored, but they take their force
from their Giver and the mutual love between his creatures and himself. It is this relationship of love that
Greene continually describes, and this is what transcends
the seediness of the background, the failures of his characters, and makes him a notable Christian writer. There
is something almost medieval in the images of love, the
power to wound Christ through sin. Scobie, desolate
with human love that conflicts with religious duty, can
see "the punch-drunk head of God reeling sideways."
The emphasis is unfashionable today, even among Christians, but Greene hammers it home continually and most
notably in *The End of the Affair*. Here Sarah's conversion is so ecstatic that when Maurice reads about it in
her diary he mistakenly thinks that she has found a new
human lover: the rejected suitor is jealous of the successful one.

This God is truly a jealous God, in the terms of human
eroticism rather than Mosaic law. Sometimes the objects
of his love seem incongruous, but here again we are
judging by the standards of Ida Arnold's world of exter-

nals. Sarah was baptized as a child simply because her mother wanted to spite her father, but God does not give her up and in the end makes her into a saint whose relics work miracles of healing. Is Greene here making a mockery of baptism as if it were something mechanical and permanent in effect like an innoculation—or is he rather saying that nothing can make a mockery of God and the ways through which he has chosen to act in this world?

The oddity of relationships between people stands as an earthly type of our relationship with this very personal God. The theme of relationships is important in the modern novel, a theme much developed by British novelists such as William Golding and Iris Murdoch. People's destinies seem to be drawn together; they may not like each other, may even be disastrous for each other, but they cannot get away. Greene recognizes the truth of this both for the visible society in which his books are set and for the mystical society which he believes to lie all around it. Indeed, every Christian must be something of a Unanimist, since belief in the Incarnation links all human beings as bearers and manifestations of a nature comprehended into the Godhead. However ungodlike they may seem, there is purpose in apparently chance encounters. Wilson comes to the colony on special Government service, but his presence there helps to destroy Scobie; the private investigator employed by Maurice in *The End of the Affair* is drawn into a strange, unsought relationship with Sarah and himself; the half-breed who dogs the priest in *The Power and the Glory* is a necessary agent of his final unwilling apotheosis.

In this kind of perception, Greene is one of those

writers who have rescued the novel from Victorian melo-
drama and restored to it the dignity of tragedy. It is no
longer a question of good people who keep certain principles and bad people who break them, but a jungle of
misunderstanding and incomprehension where technical
innocence is not enough.

More than this, Greene has rescued the religious novel
from the stained-glass attitudes of tradition. Is Querry a
saint? Is Scobie saved "between the stirrup and the
ground"? What matters is not the answer but the possibility of asking the question. It is in *The Power and the
Glory* that the question is most forceful. The priest has
few apparent virtues: he is not even given the dignity of
a name all through the book. Yet he and the equally
anonymous lieutenant are protagonists in a cosmic struggle. The reality of the priest's sweating cowardice is
many times contrasted with the gilded legends of saints
which a Mexican mother is reading to her children. Yet
he stands as a representative of the Church which is
greater than he, greater than the State which condemns
him. The pious mother's husband is wise:

> "As for the Church—the Church is Padre José and
> the whisky priest—I don't know of any other. If we
> don't like the Church, well, we must leave it."

There is no picking and choosing. It is all or nothing
for the faithful, for the priest, for the lieutenant to whom
the Church is an offense in the new, tidier society. The
lieutenant is a man of principle without faith; the priest,
faithful but erring, is yet developed into an almost
Christ-like figure: the quality of his betrayal by the half-
breed is stressed by frequent references to the Mexican

custom of hanging an effigy of Judas. Greene had traveled to Mexico before writing this novel; he recorded his experiences in *The Lawless Roads,* episodes and characters from which appear thinly disguised in *The Power and the Glory.*

All this is sound doctrine, for the Church has for centuries laid down the principle that the personal unworthiness of a priest does not affect the validity of the sacraments which he administers, but that is not the whole of the story. Greene does indeed show that the Church may find her real power and glory when stripped of external honor, but is there not a certain lack of balance in his work? A stranger to our culture might well get the impression from his novels that the Church is honored only by her sinners, that priests are usually bad and at best incompetent. There is much of suffering, "The only means we have to put ourselves in touch with the whole human condition," as Querry says in *A Burnt-Out Case,* but this is only one side of the Christian image. In dogmatic terms, Greene may be said to give his readers more of the Cross than of the Resurrection.

Furthermore, that plunging into the lower depths which Greene admires in Péguy and makes many of his people imitate, is a dubious way to salvation. That nothing is beyond God's redemption is a basic certainty for Christians, but is there any merit in deliberately stretching redemption to its utmost? It is an old heresy: to sin and sin in order to accomplish a terrific repentance in the end. Secular writers have felt the same desire, like George Orwell who sought the underworld of tramps and destitutes to free himself from a social class whose ethos he had come to detest. It is a comprehensible attitude, and one which has indeed formed saints, but is

more often masochistic, or a morbid excuse to go on sin-
ning, or even a terrible kind of pride. Most Christians
must try somehow to know and perform the will of God
in a round of daily failures and recoveries, none of them
very grand for good or evil.

Still, sainthood is a fact of Christian history and experience, even if masochism and morbidity are not always absent from the making of a saint. When Greene
goes to the extremes of conduct in order to demonstrate
that nothing is outside God's grace, it is worth remember-
ing that Jesus was condemned as a sinner and a criminal.
We may tend to look for him too readily in the cleaned
image that seems to us a fitting object of reverence; and
as we learn more clearly what needs to be condemned in
ourselves, it takes something near to saintliness to avoid
condemning the same things in others. To condemn and
to refrain from condemnation is one of the great and
necessary Christian paradoxes. Scobie and Querry know
only too well the answers that a confessor would give to
their problems; they recognize the decay in themselves
underneath the respect which society pays them, just as
Pinkie is conversely forced to recognize salvation where
society has rejected:

> In an alley between two shops, an old woman sat
> upon the ground; he could just see the rotting and
> discoloured face: it was like the sight of damnation.
> Then he heard the whisper: "Blessed art thou
> among women," saw the grey fingers fumbling at
> the beads. This was not one of the damned; he
> watched with horrified fascination: this was one of
> the saved.

These images of the fact that nothing is outside God's

power and love need cause no difficulty to any thinking Christian. But Greene has provided a bigger stumbling block which has tripped up some of his greatest admirers. What can be said of the bargaining prayers, the bartering which God seems to accept? Sarah promises to give up Maurice if he does not die (it is possible to read the passage as meaning that he is actually restored from death to life), and she keeps her side of the bargain and attains a kind of sainthood. Scobie asks God to take away his peace forever but to give peace to the child suffering after shipwreck: the child immediately receives the peace of death and Scobie begins his path toward despair and suicide. The Mexican priest prays to be caught because he is afraid of the life forced on him, and he is betrayed and trapped and executed. In Greene's play *The Potting Shed,* a priest actually prays for the return to life of a nephew who has hanged himself, asking God to take away his own faith in return, and the bargain is fulfilled in both respects.

This kind of thing at first seems repellent. To make bargains about divinity is the sin of Judas, even if we know too well that Christians often try to make bargains with God and store up bits of spiritual credit to balance against some wished-for sin. Is Greene so badly instructed in the Catholic faith as to suppose that this is sound and acceptable doctrine? Clearly not, and clearly a man who has thought so long and deeply about the imaginative presentation of that faith must know what he is saying. It would seem that in this, the farthest extreme of all, he is again saying that nothing can alienate from God those whom he has chosen, that nothing is beyond his mercy. The stark bargain, which the Christian sees as blasphemy and the unbeliever as a proof of the inadequacy of professed faith, even this may become an instrument of grace. You cannot turn away God even by offering your thirty pieces of silver: he may accept them and save you in spite of yourself. Henry Miles in *The End of the Affair* admits how as a schoolboy he prayed to get into the football team:

> "I'm afraid that kind of prayer isn't much good, is it, father?"
>
> "Any sort's better than none. It's a recognition of God's power anyway, and that's a kind of praise, I suppose."

In an age when we have learned to fear extremism, when its political manifestations have too often driven men of goodwill to other extremes that turn out as badly, we may be grateful to a writer who offers us a church more revolutionary, more destructive of polite, conventional thinking, than anything that Karl Marx ever dreamed up. Christianity has been for too long equated with the idea of safety, of the Establishment. We need to be reminded that the first Christians were rebels, dangerous radicals, "they who have turned the world upside down."

The turning upside down that Greene has done is his contribution to modern literature. He has given us Christian stories that are truly adventure stories: exciting narrative in the tradition of John Buchan, Anthony Hope, and A. E. W. Mason, but with a difference. He has a power of storytelling reminiscent of R. L. Stevenson, with whose family he is connected; and the dualism which Greene sees and describes in human nature is perhaps not surprising from one with the same blood as the author of *Weir of Hermiston* and *Doctor Jekyll and Mr. Hyde.* His similarity to Henry James in his use of imagery has already been noted, and Jamesian too is his use of the "shifting point of view" which enriches his presentation of character. But Greene is ultimately beyond discussion of "influences." He is not a great innovator in the form of the novel, yet he is not fully within any single tradition. If he shows a line of descent in English literature, it is rather from the morality plays. He takes those themes of human life which for many people remain forever in the gray realms of abstraction, and makes them visible. He parades theological ideas under the guise of suffering, striving, individual men and women.

The world is perplexed, more perhaps than ever before, by the need for choice. Greene reminds us, in the true existentialist manner, that we choose continually in every moment, making a choice even when we seem to refuse to make one. In a world which has received the Christian revelation, every choice is made for or against its claims. There is no compulsion, no rescinding of free will, but neither is there any contracting out. Graham Greene may give some headaches to conventional theologians, but he presents the situation in a way which fallible, grubby, seedy people like us can well recognize as being close to our own.

SELECTED BIBLIOGRAPHY

A very substantial number of the major books of each of the writers discussed in this volume will be found to be currently available in inexpensive paperback editions which are conveniently indexed in *Paperbound Books in Print,* published by the R. R. Bowker Company (1180 Avenue of the Americas, New York, N. Y. 10036).

The following critical studies are recommended:

KAFKA

Günther Anders, *Franz Kafka,* trans. by A. Steer and A. K. Thorlby. London: Bowes & Bowes Ltd., 1960. (In the series "Studies in Modern European Literature and Thought," ed. by Erich Heller.)

Max Brod, *Franz Kafka: A Biography.* New York: Schocken Books, 1947.

Albert Camus, *The Myth of Sisyphus and Other Essays,* trans. by Justin O'Brien. New York: Alfred A. Knopf, 1955. Pp. 124-138.

Angel Flores, ed., *The Kafka Problem.* New York: New Directions, 1946.

Angel Flores and Homer Swander, eds., *Franz Kafka Today.* Madison: University of Wisconsin Press, 1958.

Ronald Gray, *Kafka's Castle.* Cambridge: Cambridge University Press, 1956.

Erich Heller, *The Disinherited Mind.* Philadelphia: Dufour and Saifer, 1952. Pp. 157-181.

Heinz Politzer, *Parable and Paradox: A Study of Franz Kafka.* Ithaca: Cornell University Press, 1962.

Nathan A. Scott, Jr., *Rehearsals of Discomposure: Alienation and Reconciliation in Modern Literature.* New York: King's Crown Press of Columbia University Press, 1952. Pp. 11-65.

Herbert Tauber, *Franz Kafka,* trans. by G. Humphreys Roberts and Roger Senhouse. New Haven: Yale University Press, 1948.

Rebecca West, *The Court and the Castle.* New Haven: Yale University Press, 1957.

HEMINGWAY

Carlos H. Baker, ed., *Hemingway and His Critics.* New York: Hill and Wang, 1961.

Carlos H. Baker, *Hemingway: The Writer as Artist.* Princeton: Princeton University Press, 1961.

John Killinger, *Hemingway and the Dead Gods*. Lexington: University of Kentucky Press, 1960.

John K. McCaffery, ed., *Ernest Hemingway: The Man and His Work*. Cleveland: World Publishing Co., 1950.

Earl H. Rovit, *Ernest Hemingway*. New York: Twayne Publishers, 1963.

Stewart Sanderson, *Hemingway*. Edinburgh: Oliver & Boyd, 1961.

Robert Percy Weeks, ed., *Hemingway*. Englewood Cliffs, N. J.: Prentice-Hall, 1962.

Philip Young, *Ernest Hemingway*. New York: Rinehart, 1952.

CAMUS

Germaine Brée, *Camus*. New Brunswick: Rutgers University Press, 1961.

John Cruickshank, *Albert Camus and the Literature of Revolt*. London and New York: Oxford University Press, 1959.

R. W. B. Lewis, *The Picaresque Saint*. Philadelphia: J. B. Lippincott Co., 1959. Pp. 57-108.

Nathan A. Scott, Jr., *Albert Camus*. London: Bowes & Bowes Ltd., 1962. (In the series "Studies in Modern European Literature and Thought," ed. by Erich Heller.)

Philip Thody, *Albert Camus: A Study of His Work*. London: Hamish Hamilton, 1957.

GREENE

Kenneth Allott and Miriam Farris, *The Art of Graham Greene*. London: Hamish Hamilton, 1951.

Francis L. Kunkel, *The Labyrinthine Ways of Graham Greene*. New York: Sheed & Ward, 1959.

R. W. B. Lewis, *The Picaresque Saint*. Philadelphia: J. B. Lippincott Co., 1959. Pp. 220-274.

Donat O'Donnell, *Maria Cross: Imaginative Patterns in a Group of Modern Catholic Writers*. New York: Oxford University Press, 1952. Pp. 63-91.

Nathan A. Scott, Jr., "Graham Greene: Christian Tragedian," in *Graham Greene: Some Critical Considerations*, ed. by Robert O. Evans (Lexington: University of Kentucky Press, 1963).

Philip Stratford, *Faith and Fiction: Creative Process in Greene and Mauriac*. Notre Dame: University of Notre Dame Press, 1964.

Morton Dauwen Zabel, *Craft and Character in Modern Fiction*. New York: The Viking Press, 1957. Pp. 276-296.